# Learning Shell Scripting with Zsh

Your one-stop guide to reading, writing, and debugging simple and complex Z shell scripts

**Gastón Festari**

PUBLISHING

BIRMINGHAM - MUMBAI

# Learning Shell Scripting with Zsh

First published: January 2014

Production Reference: 1080114

Published by Packt Publishing Ltd.
Livery Place
35 Livery Street
Birmingham B3 2PB, UK.

ISBN 978-1-78328-293-7

www.packtpub.com

Cover Image by Aniket Sawant (aniket_sawant_photography@hotmail.com)

# Credits

**Author**
Gastón Festari

**Reviewers**
Takeshi Banse

Alice Ferrazzi

Chien-Wei Huang

**Acquisition Editor**
Rubal Kaur

**Commissioning Editor**
Govindan K

**Technical Editors**
Nikhil Potdukhe

Tarunveer Shetty

**Copy Editors**
Dipti Kapadia

Kirti Pai

**Project Coordinator**
Aboli Ambardekar

**Proofreader**
Bridget Braund

**Indexer**
Hemangini Bari

**Production Coordinator**
Alwin Roy

**Cover Work**
Alwin Roy

# About the Author

**Gastón Festari** is a scripting language enthusiast with over five years of experience and a firm believer in free, open source software. Currently working as a developer for Globant, he likes to spread the word about zsh at different meetups and events when away from the keyboard.

The number of people who deserve their name on this page for making this possible would require a book of its own, so allow me to start by apologizing if your name isn't here by saying: I owe you a hug and a big "thank you".

To my grandparents and my family for allowing me to follow my ambitions. My friends, Xeba and his wonderful family, Mathías and Eliana, Bruno, Lore, Ce, and Dan for putting up with this project of mine. Without your encouragement and support, this could have never been completed.

My colleagues, particularly Gabriel, Diego, and Ale, for their feedback and for getting me through those particularly difficult times around Chapter Four. To the technical reviewers Alice Ferrazzi, Chien-Wei Huang, and Takeshi Banse; and staff at Packt Publishing for their great suggestions and eagle-eyed corrections.

So now you know, if you don't see your name in here, come by with a frowning face, and you'll get that much-deserved hug. I promise.

So see you around and again, thank you.

# About the Reviewers

**Takeshi Banse** lives in Tokyo, Japan. He likes to write code for Linux. His e-mail address is `takebi@laafc.net`.

**Alice Ferrazzi** has been using zsh since 2011. She is currently living in Tokyo, studying Japanese at Tokyo Central Japanese Language School (TCJ) in the morning and working at MIRACLE LINUX in the afternoon.

She contributes to Gentoo and open source software in her free time. She has a wiki at `http://aliceinwire.net`.

---

Thanks for everyone's support and encouragement.

---

**Chien-Wei Huang** is a programmer from Yunlin, Taiwan. His main programming skills include C and Python, and he also has some experience of PHP/JavaScript/MongoDB/MySQL/Java/Shell. He loves developing programs to solve the problems he faces, sharing knowledge with others, and is also interested in new technologies. His ID on the Internet is `carlcarl`. You can find him on GitHub, Plurk, and many other places. He also has a blog for programming notes at `http://blog.carlcarl.me`.

# www.PacktPub.com

## Support files, eBooks, discount offers and more

You might want to visit www.PacktPub.com for support files and downloads related to your book.

Did you know that Packt offers eBook versions of every book published, with PDF and ePub files available? You can upgrade to the eBook version at www.PacktPub.com and as a print book customer, you are entitled to a discount on the eBook copy. Get in touch with us at service@packtpub.com for more details.

At www.PacktPub.com, you can also read a collection of free technical articles, sign up for a range of free newsletters and receive exclusive discounts and offers on Packt books and eBooks.

http://PacktLib.PacktPub.com

Do you need instant solutions to your IT questions? PacktLib is Packt's online digital book library. Here, you can access, read and search across Packt's entire library of books.

## Why Subscribe?

- Fully searchable across every book published by Packt
- Copy and paste, print and bookmark content
- On demand and accessible via web browser

## Free Access for Packt account holders

If you have an account with Packt at www.PacktPub.com, you can use this to access PacktLib today and view nine entirely free books. Simply use your login credentials for immediate access.

# Table of Contents

# Preface

If I had to take a wild guess, I'd say that you are reading these lines because, like me, you spend quite some time dealing with Unix systems. Be it because your job requires you to, or you simply love to poke around an operating system's internals, the shell is arguably how you deal with most of your activities.

Historically, shells were conceived for speeding up our work, but we all know that at some point, what was supposed to be a leaner way to get things done turned into a slugfest of arcane symbols and impossibly long-to-remember lines of code.

Wouldn't it be great then, if we could squeeze just a bit more out of our system? Imagine the things you are currently doing and being able to do them in a more efficient, elegant way, even the things that you thought were some sort of magic that only Linux's wizards with centuries' worth of experience were able to perform.

What if I told you that feats such as knowing which option flags are available to a program no longer require you to scan endless screens of manpages? Imagine not having to deal with journeys along infinite horizontal lines of characters anymore. And what about relying on automatic completion instead of typing the same lines again? What if knowing which directory you are currently working on merely required you to stare at your command prompt? Now imagine that all it takes for getting started with all of this only demands you to switch to a new shell.

## What this book covers

*Chapter 1, Getting Started*, starts from scratch by explaining how to install and set up zsh. Learn about startup files and customizing the shell prompt.

*Chapter 2, Alias and History*, explains how aliasing works, how to define aliases in your startup files, and teaches you how to work with the shell's history log.

*Chapter 3, Advanced Editing*, introduces zsh's Line Editor and working with the various shortcuts and key bindings on the command line.

*Chapter 4, Globbing*, introduces the new ways of working with the system's files and directories by applying parameter substitution and modifiers to deal with all kinds of tasks.

*Chapter 5, Completion*, introduces you to one of zsh's greatest features and shows you how to start tweaking "the new" completion system by defining your own styles and functions.

*Chapter 6, Tips and Tricks*, explains miscellaneous settings and configuration options that are definitely worth trying, together with some cool community projects that should be on your radar.

# What you need for this book

Before getting started, you should be comfortable in handling a terminal emulator. Most operating systems bundle such software within their stock set of applications, but as is the case with any application, there are other offerings out there waiting to be discovered. Such alternatives are probably even better suited for the task at hand, so please make sure you get to know the ins and outs of your weapon of choice and its quirks before jumping into this book.

Also required for following this text and the provided examples is the Git source code management system. It can be easily obtained and installed by following the instructions provided at http://git-scm.com, and it's an indispensable tool when attempting to use some of the various software projects and sources mentioned throughout this book.

# Who this book is for

This book is great for system administrators, developers, and other computer professionals involved with Unix, who are looking to improve on their daily tasks involving the Unix shell. It's assumed that you have some familiarity with a Unix command-line interface and feel comfortable with editors such as Emacs or vi. The usage of web browsers is optionally required for reading some online documentation.

# Conventions

In this book, you will find a number of styles of text that distinguish between different kinds of information. Here are some examples of these styles, and an explanation of their meaning.

Code words in text are shown as follows: "This alias changes the behavior of ls by calling it with the color flag every time you type it, instead of using its more vanilla version."

A block of code is set as follows:

```
zstyle ':completion:*:descriptions' format '%B%d%b'
zstyle ':completion:*:messages' format %d
zstyle ':completion:*:warnings' format 'No matches for: %d'
```

When we wish to draw your attention to a particular part of a code block, the relevant lines or items are set in bold:

```
autoload -Uz compinit
compinit
```

Any command-line input or output is written as follows:

```
$ zsh --version
zsh 5.0.2 (x86_64-apple-darwin12.3.0)
```

**New terms** and **important words** are shown in bold. Words that you see on the screen, in menus or dialog boxes for example, appear in the text like this: "Should your operating system greet you with a polite **zsh not found** message, that's ok though; otherwise, you won't be reading these lines."

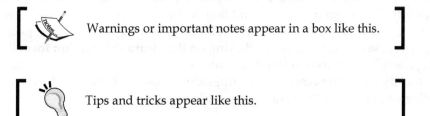

Warnings or important notes appear in a box like this.

Tips and tricks appear like this.

# Reader feedback

Feedback from our readers is always welcome. Let us know what you think about this book—what you liked or may have disliked. Reader feedback is important for us to develop titles that you really get the most out of.

To send us general feedback, simply send an e-mail to feedback@packtpub.com, and mention the book title through the subject of your message.

If there is a topic that you have expertise in and you are interested in either writing or contributing to a book, see our author guide on www.packtpub.com/authors.

# Customer support

Now that you are the proud owner of a Packt book, we have a number of things to help you to get the most from your purchase.

## Downloading the example code

You can download the example code files for all Packt books you have purchased from your account at http://www.packtpub.com. If you purchased this book elsewhere, you can visit http://www.packtpub.com/support and register to have the files e-mailed directly to you.

## Errata

Although we have taken every care to ensure the accuracy of our content, mistakes do happen. If you find a mistake in one of our books—maybe a mistake in the text or the code—we would be grateful if you would report this to us. By doing so, you can save other readers from frustration and help us improve subsequent versions of this book. If you find any errata, please report them by visiting http://www.packtpub. com/support, selecting your book, clicking on the **errata submission form** link, and entering the details of your errata. Once your errata are verified, your submission will be accepted and the errata will be uploaded to our website, or added to any list of existing errata, under the Errata section of that title.

# Piracy

Piracy of copyright material on the Internet is an ongoing problem across all media. At Packt, we take the protection of our copyright and licenses very seriously. If you come across any illegal copies of our works, in any form, on the Internet, please provide us with the location address or website name immediately so that we can pursue a remedy.

Please contact us at copyright@packtpub.com with a link to the suspected pirated material.

We appreciate your help in protecting our authors, and our ability to bring you valuable content.

# Questions

You can contact us at questions@packtpub.com if you are having a problem with any aspect of the book, and we will do our best to address it.

# 1
# Getting Started

So, what's the deal with Z shell? You probably have a solid notion of what to expect from a modern shell, so things such as command history, completion, and autocorrection will not wow you as much as someone who just discovered Bash. However, unlike some of the other available shells out there, Z shell (zsh) boasts of a really powerful scripting language and an incredible completion system. Actually, incredible doesn't even begin to describe it. Swift and effortless sounds a bit more appropriate. Zsh also incorporates—and arguably, improves on—many of the useful features of Bash, ksh, and csh, even going so far as to allow you to emulate these shells in your scripts for an extra layer of compatibility.

Once you discover things such as multiline editing or start relying on automatic spell correction though, I promise you will look back at your old days of keyboard mashing buttons and wonder why you didn't make the switch sooner. So let's get started with it, shall we?

In this chapter, we will start by getting to know zsh, with a quick glimpse at some of the features that make it unique. Before we embark on our adventure though, we will need to install and configure our new shell, so we can ensure everything is up and running smoothly. We then move on to the configuration—what are the startup files, and how to use the different styles, escape sequences, and conditional expressions in order to customize the prompt.

## Installing zsh

Like most things on your system, zsh needs to be installed and maintained; so, in this section we will learn how to do that. Note though, in order to avoid introducing inconsistencies and/or incompatibilities into your operating system, the recommended way of installing zsh is straight from your package maintainer's available sources. Either refer to your system's documentation or head to zsh's home page (http://zsh.sourceforge.net) to learn more about the whole installation procedure.

Before getting started, it would be a good idea to check whether you will need to install or update your current installation of zsh, as the package could already be installed on some Unix systems. So, open up your favorite terminal emulator and type in the following command:

```
$ echo $SHELL
```

This should print out something like /bin/sh or /bin/bash on most systems, and this means that your current login shell is something other than zsh. If you see zsh in the result though, go ahead and call the following commands:

```
$ zsh --version
zsh 5.0.2 (x86_64-apple-darwin12.3.0)
```

With some luck (and a healthy regime of system updates on your side, of course), you should see zsh's version, something that pretty much resembles the previous snippet. If that's the case, you can go ahead and skip this section. Should your operating system greet you with a polite **zsh not found** message. That's ok though, otherwise you wouldn't be reading these lines. Let's get into the installation part of the deal, shall we?

We'll use the latest stable release—version 5.0.2 as at the time of writing this book—as a reference in this book. So it is advisable to try and update your current installation if you are running a previous release. Refer to your package manager's documentation in order to update zsh.

# Installing on Linux

Depending on which distribution of Linux your PC is currently sporting, zsh might (or might not) be in its repositories or, better yet, already installed on your OS. You should always refer to your OS's package listing in the rare event that zsh is unavailable.

On Debian and its multitude of derived distributions—such as Ubuntu and Linux Mint—you could get the whole installation process completed by simply opening a terminal and running the following commands:

```
$ sudo apt-get update
$ sudo apt-get install zsh
```

Depending on your flavor of Debian and its repositories, you could get any version of zsh ranging from 4.3.x to 5.0.0 and upwards (if using any current release, at least). Again, try to stick to the latest and greatest whenever possible.

You can always check the version of zsh by running `zsh --version` in the terminal.

Red Hat-based distributions such as Fedora will need you to input the following commands:

```
$ sudo yum check-update
$ sudo yum install zsh
```

Then, there are the openSuSE users:

```
$ sudo zypper refresh
$ sudo zypper install zsh
```

And let's not forget the Arch users:

```
$ sudo pacman -S zsh
```

Wait for the download and installation scripts/triggers to complete, go ahead, and skip to the next section.

# Installing on OS X

Arguably, the easiest way to get your hands on zsh in OS X is either via Homebrew (`http://www.brew.sh`) or MacPorts (`http://www.macports.org`), package managers that aim to extend the default options available to OS X users. Unfortunately, neither of these options come bundled with OS X. You will need to install either of the solutions before you can go ahead and make do with the latest version of zsh (which remains 5.0.2 at the time of writing this book). So, open your terminal emulator of preference, and either type:

```
$ brew install zsh
```

or

```
$ sudo port install zsh
```

Wait for the download and installation scripts to finish, and then go ahead and jump straight into the next section. Also, refer to the documentation of each application in order to troubleshoot any kind of problems that could come up during the installation of the package.

# Compiling from source

The official home for zsh is located at `zsh.sourceforge.net`, and this is where you should point your browser in order to get started with your building adventure. Keep in mind, though, that the recommended way of obtaining a zsh binary for your system is via the compiled binaries packages. If for some reason, however, you just want to get the latest and greatest and don't mind dealing with more bugs than those of a stable release, you most likely will need to clone the repo using the Git version control software:

```
$ git clone git://git.code.sf.net/p/zsh/code zsh
```

Make sure you check-out and track the master branch, which is where the latest goodies have been committed. Also, keep in mind that there are some dependencies that need to be met before you can build your fresh local copy of zsh. These are all well-documented in the many configuration files that have been cloned into your disk, so take a long, hard look at the README file before you attempt things such as building the configure script.

> Installing Git on your platform of choice goes beyond the scope of this book, but be rest assured that you won't have trouble following the instructions at `http://www.git-scm.com`.

# First run

Now that zsh is on your system, how about we take it for a spin? Go ahead and open your terminal emulator of choice and call the following command:

```
$ zsh
```

Like many other applications these days, zsh has a first-run wizard (bear with me, it almost resembles one). This is one of those magic creatures whose sole purpose is to help us configure our tools on a swift swoop of questions and decision making. We'll skip the new user configuration this time, but feel free to choose whatever method works best for you, taking the question-by-question approach or just pressing *Q* on your keyboard to abort the operation. Just remember that the `newuser` module is called from `<zshInstallFolder>/Functions/Newuser/zsh-newuser-install` or `<zshInstallFolder>/functions/zsh-newuser-install` in OS X—should you require its services in the future.

In order to avoid having to skip the configuration options on each subsequent run, you can go ahead and create what is known as a *startup file*:

```
% touch ~/.zshrc
```

We just created our main preferences file; the problem is, it stands empty as it is. Let's go ahead and add some preferences, shall we?

There will be plenty of references to zsh's options — the various settings that alter the shell's behavior — thus, now is as good a time as any to establish a couple of conventions. Firstly, the naming scheme is somewhat too forgiving — it is case-insensitive and ignores underscores and ignores underscores. As such, both the following option names mean the same.

SOME_OPTION and SOMEOPTION

Secondly, try to think of options as *switches*. As the name implies, they can either be turned *on* or *off*. Of the many ways that zsh provides to toggle its options, it is arguably easier to remember the setopt/unsetopt combo.

setopt SOME_OPTION # enables any option.

unsetopt SOME_OPTION # use this to disable an option.

Conversely, you can negate the behavior of an option by prepending NO to its name, thus making unsetopt SOME_OPTION mean the same as setopt NO_SOME_OPTION or, keeping in mind that underscores are only there for human readability, the same as setopt NOSOMEOPTION.

Just for sanity's sake and because I do love me some standards, we'll use ALL_CAPS_SNAKE_CASE for the options in this book.

Open ~/.zshrc with your favorite editor; you can use editors such as vim, Emacs, nano, or whatever kids find cool these days, and add the following line:

```
autoload -U promptinit # initialize the prompt system promptinit
```

Let's go over what we just typed: the first line of the code is our way to tell the shell to start its promptinit module — a series of functions that deal with handling the shell's various prompts and functionality. What you see right after the hash sign is just a comment to remind you of what the command is doing and why it is there. Finally, the last line is the one that actually calls and initializes the prompt module. It might not seem much, but it will come in handy when dealing with prompts, I promise.

Feel free to omit the comments and make sure you save your changes.

Zsh will ignore each line that starts with a hash (#) — or pound — sign. This is really helpful for debugging preferences and, better yet, documenting your functionality. Consider the next example, with comments in bold:

```
# This is a comment and will be ignored by the shell.
HISTFILE=~/.zsh_history # sets the location of the
history file
```

# Making zsh your login shell

If there's something that shells take seriously, is their role. See, the thing with shells is that they like to hang out in very specific categories — they are either interactive or non-interactive, and then there are login shells.

As you might have guessed from their name, *interactive shells* allow you to interact with them; that is, they display a prompt, you enter a command, and they get back to you with an answer and a prompt that is ready for new input. On the other hand, Apply interactive shells get called to execute a script and go off their own merry way when the job is done.

Put simply, a prompt usually is the blinking cursor that tells you a shell is ready for you.

What about login shells then? Well, unlike interactive shells, *login shells* are usually called when the user performs a login — be it either on the local machine or when using tools such as SSH, for example — and takes the trouble to go through your startup files and configuration bits and pieces of the shell. More importantly, your login shell doesn't necessarily need to be interactive.

In the previous section, we used a direct call to the binary zsh to start zsh. As you can imagine, this is but a temporary workaround, as typing the name of the shell every single time we want to use it seems a bit impractical, to say the least. Even worse is the thought of having your previous shell lurking beneath and ready to jump back at you as soon as you're done with zsh. If you don't trust me, go ahead and type exit; I'll wait. See that thing that's on your screen? That's your former command-line companion right there. Say your goodbyes and hop back into zsh by typing zsh and pressing *return*.

So what comes next is — you guessed it — getting rid of that old shell of yours and saving yourself the trouble of remembering to call zsh each time you want to use it.

You can always trick zsh, and many other shells, into thinking it is a login shell by starting it with either the `-l` or `--login` flag. Open your terminal and type either of the following commands:

```
$ zsh -l
```

or

```
$ zsh --login
```

Voilà! A shell with a login complex.

Luckily for us, the Unix `chsh` command seems to be just what the doctor recommended, so go ahead and type the following in your terminal:

```
$ chsh -s $(which zsh)
```

In the previous snippet, we're telling the system to change the shell for the current user. The option `-s` is used here to specify the location of the shell binary. That fancy `$()` construct you see there is our way of telling the shell to expand the result of the command within the parentheses, which is the result of the command `which zsh`.

You might recall `which` from the previous section, when we required its services to figure out the location of our existing zsh installation. The job of `which` consists of shouting out loud the location of any program file in the user's `$PATH` environment variable. Thus, we can safely assume that if zsh is not there, something has taken a wrong turn somewhere and, perhaps, it's advisable to retrace our steps.

It's more than likely that changing your login shell will require it to run with elevated privileges, so make sure you are using an account with the appropriate permissions.

From now on, you'll be greeted by zsh by default on your system and every time you start your terminal emulator of choice. And likely so, you have installed and made zsh your login shell. Next up is tweaking it.

# Shell options

Besides tricking zsh into thinking it's a login shell with the `-l` flag, there are many other helpful options you can set when invoking it. Namely, `zsh -v` will switch on the verbose mode, which will make the shell print out any line before it gets executed. Then, there's `zsh -x`—for `xtrace`—which can prove invaluable when debugging your scripts, or `zsh -f` that will start a clean instance of zsh using the default settings.

Any of these options can also be set after the shell has been started; you simply have to call the desired option flag via the `set` command. The following example triggers the verbose mode on a running session:

```
% set -v
% echo 'quite the echo in here'
> echo 'quite the echo in here'
> 'quite the echo in here'
```

**Downloading the example code**

You can download the example code files for all Packt books you have purchased from your account at http://www.packtpub.com. If you purchased this book elsewhere, you can visit http://www.packtpub.com/support and register to have the files e-mailed directly to you.

And, you can disable any option with the same `set` command and replacing the dash/minus sign with a plus sign as follows:

```
# disables verbose mode
% set +v
```

More info regarding the various shell options and their usage can be found in the `zshoptions(1)` manpage (`man zshoptions`).

# The startup files

Like most login shells, zsh relies on a series of configuration files known as *startup* files, which contain the commands and preferences to be executed and set during the shell startup routine. We used the `.zshrc` file in the previous sections to avoid being bothered by the `newuser` function, but now that we have made zsh our login shell, it's time we take a closer look at what we can do with them.

By default, zsh looks for startup files in the user's home directory, `$HOME` (or its alias, the more popular tilde, `~`. We'll alternate their use in this text as the path to the current user's home folder on the system), environment variable. You can tell zsh to look for your configuration files in another folder by setting the parameter ZDOTDIR to a directory of your choice in your `.zshenv` file under `$HOME`:

```
ZDOTDIR=/etc/my_kewl_folder/.zshrc
```

During startup, zsh looks for, or *sources*, a very specific system and user set of filenames under /etc/. Right after this, each of these files have a user-editable doppelganger, typically located in $HOME, which gets read. There are some rules, however, that might make zsh skip some of these files altogether. The ordering of these files is really important, as setting an option in the wrong file can result in commands getting executed at the wrong time and some really funky behavior. Thus, try to keep in mind the following order when setting preferences on your files:

- zshenv
- zprofile
- zshrc
- zlogin

If zsh is not called as an interactive shell, zprofile and zshrc together with their counterparts in $HOME (~/.zprofile and ~/.zshrc) will not be sourced. In addition, if zsh is not called as a login shell, zlogin and $HOME/.zlogin will also be skipped.

 Depending on how you installed zsh, another directory besides /etc/ can be used when looking for the global files.

Typically, you'd only like to mess with your own user's preferences, so we'll focus on the startup files that reside under $HOME, those are as follows:

- ~/.zshenv: This will be called immediately after /etc/zshenv. You should only add things such as the PATH settings and stuff you want to make available to any type of shell, whether it's interactive or not.
- ~/.zprofile: This is the companion to /etc/zprofile and kind of the boring guy out of the startup files bunch. You should put here any scripts you want executed before ~/.zshrc.
- ~/.zshrc: This is your workhorse. Most of your user settings and shell preferences end up here. Keep in mind it'll only be taken into account for interactive shells. As we'll see later on, you can declutter and expand its reach by sourcing multiple files.
- ~/.zlogin: This will be executed right after ~/.zshrc and works pretty much like ~/.zprofile, so you should put the scripts that you want called after your main startup file here.

On the opposite corner of the startup files, there are the *shutdown* files. As you can imagine, this relatively smaller set of files gets called not only in a specific order but also during the logout sequence of the login shell. The shutdown files can be considered a subset of the startup files, so there's no need to lose sleep over them. The important thing to remember is that when you type `logout` in the command line, the settings stored in the user configurable `~/.zlogout` file are read, followed by the installation file `/etc/zlogout`.

You can use the options RCS and GLOBAL_RCS to disable the loading mechanism of the startup files. This preference has to be unset on the system file `/etc/zshenv` as follows:

```
unset RCS # disables loading of files other than zshenv
unset GLOBAL_RCS # disables loading of files under /etc/
```

For instance, if the RCS option is unset in `zshenv` (the first file that is read), `~/.zshenv` and all the remaining files will be skipped. Keep in mind though, that both of these options can be turned on again by any subsequent file that you load.

For example, if you have the following in `/etc/shenv`:

```
unset RCS
source my_options_file.zsh
```

And then in `my_options_file.zsh` add:

```
# some more options here
set RCS
```

Then, the shell will proceed and load `.zshenv` as if nothing happened. So, be careful!

We have taken a look at the startup files and their somewhat strict ordering; now, it's time we get up close and personal with the prompt.

# The shell prompt

Give anyone enough time with a shell and, inevitably, the question of "how do I add colors to it?" is bound to come up. Luckily though, zsh boasts a truckload of configuration options and escape sequences that will let you do just that and even more. In this section, we'll delve into the nuts and bolts of options at your disposal to customize the prompt.

# The prompt command

Zsh comes with a wide array of predefined prompt configurations that can be used as building blocks for something that more adequately meets your needs. Among other things, the utility `prompt` allows you to select your preferred theme. On a default installation, the various themes and user contributions are located under `<zshFolder>/Functions/Prompts` (or `<zshFolder>/functions` in OS X) and follow the naming scheme `prompt_<theme>_setup`. To have a look at what's included in the stock package, just type the following command:

```
$ prompt -p
```

And you should see a list of all the available prompt themes included with zsh. You can use the `-p` option together with a theme name to take a closer look at any of the themes:

```
$ prompt -p
```

In order to use the `prompt` function, you will need to set up the `promptinit` module on your shell. The easiest way to do this is to add it to your `.zshrc` file. Take a look at the section *First run* if you haven't done so yet.

> You can refer to the *PROMPT THEMES* section under the `zshcontrib(1)` manpage in order to get more in-depth information regarding prompts on zsh. Just type `man zshcontrib` in your terminal to get started.

You can test drive any theme you like, applying it temporarily to your current shell by typing:

```
$ prompt <theme_name>
```

Some themes, such as `adam1`, can even accept some extra configuration parameters like the following:

```
$ prompt adam1 red yellow magenta # sets the 'adam1' theme
```

By default, zsh won't be too fond of comments typed in the command line. Luckily, you can alter this behavior by setting the following option in your `.zshrc` file:

```
setopt INTERACTIVE_COMMENTS   # allow inline comments like this one
```

In the previous snippet, we are passing a list of options to the theme, namely the colors `red`, `yellow`, and `magenta`. You can get a more thorough description of what's allowed for each prompt theme by calling the built-in help on any given theme:

```
$ prompt -h <theme_name>
```

Try this on your favorite themes and see what else can be tweaked out of them.

Once you have found a combination that suits you, you can go ahead and commit to those changes. Just open your `.zshrc` file with your editor and add the following line:

```
autoload -U promptinit
promptinit
prompt adam1 red yellow magenta
```

We took our previous preferences file and sparkled some color in the default prompt `adam1`. So, how about we tweak it to make it feel more like home?

 If you have invested a fair amount of time on customizing your prompt in your previous shell, it can be quite a headache trying to figure out the different rules set, so it can be ported to zsh. Luckily, zsh provides a series of tools for making the switch a more or less smooth experience. Located under `<zshFolder>/Misc`, you can use the `bash2zshprompt` or `c2z` scripts to migrate your Bash or csh preferences respectively. Note, however, that some distributions might be missing this, in which case you should head straight to the official repo and get your hands on a local copy. See the *Compiling from source* section for more information on how to get the zsh source code.

# Customizing the prompt

Zsh boasts five different prompts you can tweak, each with its specific purpose. Although you probably won't have to worry about dealing with them in most usage scenarios, it is, nevertheless, important that we get to know their role. For a more detailed description of each of them, I suggest you take a look at `man zshmisc`.

Zsh likes to refer to its main prompt variable as $PS1 or its alias, $PROMPT (also $prompt). Rest assured though, both (actually the three of them, that is) are the same beast and are treated equally by zsh. Then there's $RPS1 that prints a prompt at the right-hand side of the screen. Unlike other prompts though, it automatically disappears whenever line width is needed.

$PS2 gets displayed whenever the shell is waiting for more input, such as at the start of some unfinished syntactic structure or when you add inline comments to the command line. $PS3 is used for making choices within a select loop control mechanism. Last but not the least, $PS4 really comes in handy for debugging scripts.

Overall, these are the set of tools we will be working with, extending their functionality beyond the basics with a nifty set of tools known as escape sequences.

> You can use the source command to reload your zsh configuration files at any time. Just save your changes and call the following command:
>
> ```
> $ source file_path/file_name
> ```
>
> Remember to use double quotes if your file path includes spaces.
>
> ```
> $ source "random folder/.zshenv"
> ```

# Using escape sequences

Escape sequences are a set of predefined information shortcuts that can be added to zsh's prompt settings. They can show information such as the name of the machine to which you are logged on, the current date and time of the system, and even the current working directory. Most escape sequences are defined with a modulo or percent (%) operator, and some of them even take optional parameters to extend their functionality further.

For the magic to happen, however, we first need to add a new setting to our preferences file. Open .zshrc and add the following line:

```
setopt PROMPT_SUBST
```

By doing this, we're enabling the PROMPT_SUBST option. This will make zsh treat $PROMPT just as if it were a vanilla shell variable, and it will be checked against for command substitution, parameter and arithmetic expansion.

Next, we'll go through many of the available escape sequences and their meanings. Keep in mind that this is by no means a complete list of all the available options; as such, you can always refer to the zshmisc(1) manpage—particularly, the section titled *Prompt Expansion*—should you need a more comprehensive listing of the available options.

# Shell state options

The following options serve as indicators for some aspects of the current state of the shell:

- %#: This displays # if the shell is running with elevated privileges and displays % otherwise
- %?: This shows the exit status code of the last command executed
- %h or %!: This shows the current history event number
- %L: This displays the current value of the $SHLVL variable
- %j: This prints the number of jobs being executed

# Login information options

The following options display more useful information about the host and machine on which the shell is currently running:

- %M: This shows the machine's *hostname*.
- %m: Same as the previous. Hostname is printed up to the first dot (.) separator. It takes an optional integer after % for the number of components to be displayed.
- %n: This will have the same effect as printing environment variable $USERNAME.

# Directory options

The following options provide information regarding the path of the current working directory ($PWD) and filesystem directories:

- %d or %/: This shows the current directory. Works just as printing the $PWD environment variable.
- %~: Same as the previous, but if the current directory is $HOME, ~ is displayed instead.
- %c or %.: This lists the amount of directories trailing $PWD. It takes an integer as the parameter after %. Thus, %2c would show the two preceding directories to $PWD.
- %C: Same as the previous, but directory names are not replaced with any symbols.

# Date and time options

The following options provide miscellaneous date and time information:

- `%D`: This prints the current system date in the `yy-mm-dd` format.
- `%W`: Same as the previous but in `mm/dd/yy` format.
- `%w`: This shows the date in `day-dd` format.
- `%T`: This displays the current time of the day, 24-hour format.
- `%t` or `%@`: Same as the previous, uses a 12-hour, am/pm format.
- `%*`: Same as the previous, also displays seconds.

# Text formatting options

Unlike the previous escape sequences, these need to be opened and closed around the desired part of the prompt. That is, in order to underline word, you need to type it as `%Uword%u`. Pay special attention to the difference in the case of the opening (UPPERCASE) and closing (lowercase) escape sequences, as shown in the following points:

- `%U` `%u`: This enables underline mode.
- `%B` `%b`: This enables boldface mode.
- `%K` `%k`: This sets the background color. Use it as `%K{red}%k`.
- `%F` `%f`: Like the the previous, but applies to the *foreground* color.
- `%S` `%s`: This enables *standout* (highlight) mode.

When dealing with escape sequences, both `%` and `)` are somewhat special as far as zsh is concerned; thus, remember to type `%%` if you need to display a literal `%` on your prompt. Likewise, a literal `)` should be typed as `%)`. This technique is commonly referred to as *escaping characters*.

> You can enable the `PROMPT_BANG` option on your zsh configuration to use a bang (`!`) in your prompt in order to display the current history event number instead of having to escape it (`%!`). Just remember to type `!!`, should you require a literal `!`.
>
> ```
> setopt PROMPT_BANG # enables '!' substitution on prompt
> ```

# Conditional expressions

We will conclude our trip of the escape sequences by taking a look at the escape sequences available for conditional expansion. Luckily though, most of it can be summed up as the following ternary expression:

```
%(X.true-text.false-text)
```

Basically, what this means is that if the condition X is true, do whatever is in `true-text`, otherwise do whatever is in `false-text`. The important thing to remember is that you should wrap your expression with `%()`, and that the dots (`.`) you see there are completely arbitrary, meaning you can replace both of them with whatever character you like.

Regarding the `true-text`/`false-text` expressions, the manpage (as when you visit `man zshmisc`) tells us that they can be replaced with the likes of `!`. This will evaluate to true if the shell is running with privileges or `?`, which in turn can be preceded by an integer *n* and will evaluate to `true` only if the exit status of the last command matches. Thus, in order to display # as your main prompt to signal whether you are running on elevated privileges, with a bit of imagination, you can come up with things like the following:

```
PS1=%(!.#.>)
```

Likewise, you could use the following line to wrap the exit status of the last command that was run, if it was other than 0, that is:

```
PS1=%(?..(%?%))
```

# Putting it all together

As you are more than aware by now, zsh has many great features built in its prompt themes. So many in fact, that most of the time our custom solutions might feel like reinventing the wheel. We still need to take a shot at building our own prompt though; so, how about using one of the included themes as a starting point?

Navigate to your zsh installation folder or repository clone, and navigate to the Prompts folder under `Functions`. As we saw earlier, all prompts come with a setup function that follows the `prompt_<theme_name>_setup` naming pattern. Look for the setup file for the SuSE theme and open it. It will most likely be under `prompt_suse_setup`.

What you see there is a shell function that goes by the same name as the file. A single call to this `prompt_suse_setup` function, with no parameters passed, is all that it takes to make two assignments—one for the PS1 prompt and the other for PS2. Have a look at the following code, which has been formatted for this example:

```
PS1="%n@%m:%~/ > "
PS2="> "
```

So let's get started with hacking that prompt to pieces, shall we? Open your .zshrc file, and remember you will be adding the following line after the call to `promptinit`. We can start by highlighting the username, just like in the adam1 prompt:

```
PS1="%K{yellow}%n%k@%m:%~/ > "
```

If you recall from the previous section, the %K%k escape sequence defines the background color. Highlighted in the code, we wrap the escape sequence, %n, to add some background color to the current session, $USERNAME. On the right-hand side of the @ symbol remains the short version of the machine name and some fancy line indicators, of course.

Let's add an error flag to the right-hand side, so we can check immediately for an abnormal command exit code:

```
RPS1="%(?..(%?%))"
```

If you feel like it, you can test our brand-new right-hand prompt by calling a program in a way that will end abnormally. Remember, an exit status of 0 is ok; everything else will trigger our prompt. Something such as `ls some_nonexistent_folder` should be enough:

```
gfestari@machine:~/ > ls nonexistent_folder
ls: cannot access nonexistent_folder: No such file or directory
gfestari@machine:~/ >                                    (2)
```

You can sparkle some color into our right-hand prompt like we did for PS1. When you are done with your tweaking, try to leave .zshrc resembling the following code as much as possible:

```
autoload -U promptinit
promptinit

PS1="%K{yellow}%n%k@%m:%~/ > "
PS2="> "
RPS1="%(?..(%?%))"
```

We left the `autoload -U promtpinit` and `promptinit` calls in the previous example, so the prompt module would be loaded and ready for use, should you eventually require its services. Note, however, that you do not require both these calls unless you are planning on using the `prompt` module.

Save your file and let's reload zsh configuration. We do this by sourcing the `.zshrc` file one more time. Be careful though as this could take a while depending on the links to other files you might have added:

```
% source ~/.zshrc
```

 source has a leaner and meaner brother: the dot (.) alias. Now that you've met him, feel free to do things such as the following:
```
% . ~/.zshrc
```

How about we take advantage of the whole width of the terminal emulator's window? You know, because widescreen.

A particularly useful on-screen help is the current directory shortcut, which if you recall can be either `%~` or `%d`. So, how about we add a bit more context information to that lazy right-hand side prompt?

```
RPS1=%~
```

Come on, I know you didn't just think it was going to be that easy, right? We are adding functionality here, so it's not just about ditching our exit status indicator. Think about it; we need to add the current working directory to that right-hand prompt. Your first guess might be along the lines of the following command:

```
# this won't work!
RPS1=%(?..(%?%)) %~
```

This is almost perfect, save for the fact that it won't work straightaway.

```
% source .zshrc
> job not found: ~
```

Bummer! However, the slight detail that's missing is the usage of double quotes. That's right, we can sneak those spaces through the shell's string processing and come out with no errors just by using double quotes, as follows:

```
RPS1="%(?..(%?%)) %~"
```

This will tell the prompt function to take the RPS1 variable as it is and to not worry about parsing multiple parameters.

And, that's it. You have your own version of the prompt on your brand-new installation of zsh. Although, you might be wondering what's the deal with the second prompt that we left there. I'll leave it for you to decide its fate, as I really like the current old-school > indicator.

Before we are done with this chapter however, I'd like to point you towards the *PROMPT THEMES* section in the zshcontrib(1) manpage. Go ahead and type man zshcontrib on the terminal emulator of your choice for more detailed information when creating your own prompt themes.

# Summary

In this chapter, we took a head-first dive into zsh by learning the essentials regarding its features and replacing your previous login shell. We even went that extra mile and added a touch of homemade goodness by customizing the prompt with the various escape sequences and configuration options available. Just because my memory is really awful, here's a list of what's been covered so far:

- We learned how to configure and set up zsh, so we could ditch your current shell and replace it with your brand-new installation of zsh
- We met the startup files, and now we have a clear understanding of what goes on behind the curtains moments before your terminal emulator window pops up on screen
- We got acquainted with the shell prompt, and discovered that zsh offers much more than meets the eye
- We went one step further and customized the prompt after learning about escape sequences and conditional expressions

Now, your system should be all set and ready for what's left of this adventure. We still have plenty of ground to cover though, so we better get started with the next chapter, *Alias and History*, where we'll learn about the alias mechanism, how to create your own shortcuts for functions, and we'll start working with the shell's history log.

# 2
# Alias and History

In this chapter, we'll expand on the basics of zsh while focusing on aliases, one of the most time-saving features available. We'll take a closer look at how aliases work and learn to replace long, boring commands with our own short versions and automate the whole process within the startup files. We'll then move on to brace expansion, in order to avoid typing extra keystrokes whenever we can. Instead of typing the same things over again, we'll learn how to work with zsh's history and history expansion mechanisms and incorporate these new features into our workflow.

## Working with aliases

An *alias* is an alternative way of saying the same thing. Think of it as a nickname for your commands. Though, unlike the embarrassing nicknames that you might get after a party, the alias mechanism provided by your shell is a handy shortcut to a series of commands and options under a friendlier name. The whole point of an alias is to do more and, preferably, type less.

I bet I got your attention with that last "type less" part. Allow me to explain:

The `ls` command lists a directory's contents. A quick look at its manpage (`man ls`) tells us that there are quite a few options there:

```
ls -a # lists all files, even those hidden that start with a dot
ls -l # shows more information for each file, like size and
permissions
```

Using aliases we can go ahead and do something like the following:

```
% alias la='ls -a'
```

No spaces are allowed around the equals (=) sign. If the right-hand side of the assignment (that is, the part that comes after the equals) contains spaces or tabs, then make sure you use quotation marks around it as follows:

```
% alias talk='echo "quack!"'
% talk
> quack!
```

Now guess what happens if you type la? Go ahead and try it. The shell reads your alias—la in this particular case—and expands it. The whole process is similar to looking up the meaning of a word in the dictionary. Although here, once it's been found, the meaning is executed.

We can do basically the same for the -l option:

```
% alias ll='ls -l'
```

Or even mix and match as shown in the following line:

```
% alias lla='ls -laF'
```

That last snippet uses both the l and a flags together with F, meaning it behaves just the same as the -la switch, with the added option to format the output so as to easily tell files and folders apart.

Aliases apply only to interactive shells. Your shell will disable all of your existing aliases if it's being run in the non-interactive mode. Keep this in mind when creating your scripts.

You have two ways of declaring an alias. The first one is straight from the command line, as we have been doing so far. This nets you an alias which you can use instantly; the downside is that changes are only present temporarily for the duration of your current session. Close your terminal emulator or log out of the system and it goes the way of the dodo. The basic syntax for declaring an alias is as follows:

```
alias [shortname]=<longname or command(s)>
```

You can use this approach for something you'll be typing a lot but won't come back to it later. Most of the time though, we'll need something a bit more resilient. Something we can use every time we work with the command line.

Enter the startup files; if you recall from the previous chapter, startup files are read every time the shell starts, and its configuration is loaded for the current session. Kind of what the doctor recommended.

Let's open up your .zshrc then, and add the aliases we've been working on so far:

```
# put this on your .zshrc
alias la='ls -aF'
alias ll='ls -lF'
alias lla='ls -laF'
```

Save your changes, source (or use its alias, the dot (.)) your file, and aliases will be set for you to use on every future session of the shell. Despite their different behavior, both the ways of alias declaration sport the same syntax.

# Quoting characters

Any given character can be quoted by adding a \ character in front of it. This is particularly useful when dealing with "special characters" which have an additional meaning, such as $, and even an actual \ character. Take, for example, the following echo sentence:

```
# this is wrong!
% echo 'that's a quoted sentence for you'
quote>
```

The shell prompt indicates it's waiting for a quote character to be (properly) closed. The problem here is that we did not properly escape the apostrophe on "that's":

```
% echo 'that\'s a quoted sentence for you'
> that's a quoted sentence for you
```

That's all nice and working, but what happens when we have a great number of escaping to do?

```
% echo 'Escaping single quotes like this \' with backslashes \\ is really
tedious'
> Escaping single quotes like this ' with backslashes \ is really tedious
```

Luckily, zsh provides the RCQUOTES option as a workaround, which allows you to use double single quotes ('') for escaping:

```
% setopt rcquotes
% echo 'Look ma'' I''m escapin'' single quotes'
> Look ma' I'm escapin' single quotes
```

What about double quotes then? Well, these are truly special and out of the bunch, as they allow you to perform parameter and command substitution as we'll see in no time. What you have to remember when using double quotes is that either ", \, $, and ` characters need to be escaped with a backslash.

Let's give double quotes a try:

```
% echo "'echo \"\$HOME\"' will print out '$HOME'"
> 'echo "$HOME"' will print out '/Users/gfestari'
```

In the preceding example, the `$HOME` environment variable gets replaced by the actual value (`/Users/gfestari`) when the `$` character is not quoted.

You can also use backquote within double quotes for executing programs:

```
% echo "zshenv is located at: `locate zshenv`"
> zshenv is located at: /etc/zshenv
```

The shell will first execute `locate zshenv` as if it were any other command, and substitute its output within the parameters being passed to `echo`.

As you can see, you can work around single quotes' limitations for most day-to-day usage, and turn to double quotes, escape sequences, and parameter expansions whenever you have a particular need for doing so.

# Single and double quoting aliases

Single quotes (') are required when using spaces on your alias assignments; nevertheless, it's generally advisable to use them regardless of the spaces on your right-hand side. Granted, this is a "just to be safe" approach, but trust me when I say it will save you from a couple of avoidable headaches when declaring your aliases.

On the other hand, if you wish to use things such as environment variables or parameter substitution within your assignment expression (think of the prompt escape sequences we saw in the previous chapter), double quotes (") are required instead. Imagine you wish to output the current user's name with an alias. As we saw earlier, the direct way of accessing it is via the environment variable `$USERNAME`. The first thing that comes to mind then is to use the following alias:

```
# This is wrong!
alias saymyname='echo $USERNAME'
```

Unfortunately, this won't work with single quotes. The correct way of doing this is with double quotation marks as follows:

```
% alias saymyname="echo $USERNAME"
% saymyname
> gfestari
```

Complex expressions with variables generally need to be quoted, we use single quotation marks for that. If your alias requires variables to be expanded before the alias is used, go with double quotes.

As you can see, the `alias` mechanism is indeed a nifty powerful feature. If used properly, it even allows you to reshape a command's meaning:

```
% alias ls='ls --color=auto'
```

Or its equivalent on OS X:

```
% alias ls='ls -G'
```

> You can define aliases from another alias. Following the preceding example, if you do the following:
>
> ```
> alias ls='ls --color=auto'
> alias la='ls -a'
> ```
>
> The `la` alias will behave just as if you typed `ls --color=auto -a`, there's no need to type `--color=auto` again on your definition.

This alias alters the behavior of `ls` by calling it with the `color` flag every time you type it, instead of using its more vanilla version. While this comes in handy for this particular scenario, it can be really dangerous for commands such as `rm` if not used with caution.

For example, imagine what would happen if you aliased a force removal of files to `rm`:

```
# Be careful when doing things like this!
alias rm='rm -f'
```

Here you are forcing the deletion of files without a warning. What will happen is that someone, unknowingly, will execute the wrong command and end up bashing their heads on the keyboard after a mistaken deletion. The takeaway message here is that the further you stay from overriding an existing command with your "l33t alias", the better. Think of all those broken keyboards. Don't be that guy.

So, what if you don't know whether you are bypassing any of the aliases' current set for your session? Well, there's a command for that. Typing `alias` will list all the aliases for the current session:

```
% alias
> la='ls -aF'
ll='ls -lF'
lla='ls -laF'
saymyname="echo $USERNAME"
```

You can also get the information for a particular alias simply by specifying its name, as follows:

```
% alias la
> la='ls -aF'
```

And you can disable, albeit temporarily, any existing alias by typing:

```
% unalias <aliasname>
```

Simply replace `aliasname` with the name of the alias you want to turn off. This comes in really handy on those occasions when you're using a particularly strict program whose options, or even command-line syntax, is overridden by an alias.

There are a few ways by which you can prevent the shell from executing an alias that is called just as another command. Single-quoted commands and commands prepended with a backslash (\) as well as those typed as relative or absolute paths are not treated as aliases by the shell.

For example, you could use either of the following if you wish to avoid a call to an alias:

```
% 'ls'
% \ls
```

or even:

```
% /usr/bin/ls
```

Zsh also has command that will execute any argument as an external command instead of as a function or built in. Thus, you can also use it to avoid aliases. That would leave us with the following for the preceding example:

```
% command ls
```

You can get more information via `man zshbuiltins`.

As with many other things we'll be discovering throughout this book, an alias is not a golden hammer and as such, you shouldn't be aliasing willy-nilly throughout your terminal sessions. Here are a few simple considerations to keep in mind before you embark into your less-typing adventure with your pack o'aliases:

- Is my alias easier to remember? `echo -n` is way simpler than aliasing something like `echodontprinttrail`. Keep it simple, don't use aliases for the sake of it. The "Future You" will be really thankful two months from now.

- Is my alias easier to type? An awkward alias is an awful alias. Using `alias grepcola='grep --color=auto'` instead of a simpler `grep`, really? Remember: clear, concise names are awesome, but something you can't remember for the life of `ping` is not cool.

- Is my alias overriding some behavior just for the sake of it? Think of the previous `rm -f` example. Most of the time we would like to stay away from something like that; however, prompting the user each time seems like a sensible feature to add to our toolbox. Aliasing `rm='rm -i'` so the shell requires confirmation before deleting something seems a bit... nicer. Be careful with these kinds of tricks though, as relying too much on such an alias could lead to a false sense of security. That is, imagine what would happen if you get used to `rm` constantly waiting for confirmation and eventually use it recklessly on a different environment?

# Global aliases

If you enjoyed the simplicity aliases brought to the table, then global aliases are the icing on the cake. As the name implies, *global aliases* are, well, aliases that can be used anywhere, allowing you to treat filters or certain commands as a simple suffix.

Let's see some examples:

```
alias -g L='|less'
```

Pay particular attention to the `-g` option, as in a global alias.

Now you can append the `less` pager to any command's output, just by adding the `L` suffix:

```
% ls -la /etc L
```

Another option that is frequently spotted in the wild is redirecting standard error (`stderr`) and standard output (`stdout`) to `/dev/null`, so any given command can run silently:

```
alias -g NUL="> /dev/null 2>&1"
```

This will allow you to call things such as `command NUL` without the need to pollute your current terminal window with thousands of log lines and messages.

Just for the sake of clarity, never mind sticking to standards, it's advisable for you to try and define your global aliases just like your global variables, all in caps.

# Hashes

You can use a hash to give a particular directory an alias. This is particularly convenient for your workspace:

```
% echo $GOPATH
> /Users/gfestari/workspace/go
```

I don't want to type `/Users/gfestari/workspace/go` each time I want to reach the `src` folder in my `$GOPATH` directory. So how about putting hash to a good use?

```
% hash -d gosrc=$HOME/go/src
```

And now we can get there as quick as typing `cd ~gosrc` (pay attention to the leading ~ character).

Here's another example, this time using the `/var/www` directory:

```
% hash -d www=/var/www
% cd ~www
/var/www
```

You can go ahead and hash your most frequently visited directories. Just remember to add the required entries to your `.zshrc`, so you don't have to type the same thing over and over again.

For bonus points, set the `AUTO_CD` option, so you only need to input the directory's name whenever you want to change the working directories:

```
% setopt autocd
% ~www
> /var/www
```

Now go ahead and start showing off with your acquaintances, I'll wait here.

# Putting it all together

Before we move on to the next topic, here's a couple of things to try with our newly found aliases.

Raise your hand if you found yourself typing cd .. more than a few times on a terminal session. I know, I feel your pain. How about making it simpler?

We could try the following instead:

```
% alias ..='cd ..'
```

Now it's just a matter of typing . to move your current working directory up one level. Not bad, uh? We can take it a bit further:

```
alias ...='cd ../..'
alias ....='cd ../../..'
```

I'd argue that going more levels in for directory changing is pushing things a bit too far, but feel free to extend your aliases as you see fit.

What about creating directories? I bet that, like myself, more than once you saw the following:

```
% mkdir dir1/dir2
> mkdir: dir1: no such file or directory
```

This happens because dir1 doesn't exist. So what we do is—you guessed it—create an alias that allows us to automatically create the *parent* directory and also, be more verbose (as in, "list directories as they are created") about the output:

```
alias mkdir='mkdir -pv'
```

Now try to issue mkdir dir1/dir2 and see what happens. You can also apply the same switch to commands such as cp and mv, just remember to quote your assignments!

> You can use the COMPLETE_ALIASES option in your startup files in order to force the shell to treat aliases as a distinct command for completion purposes. In other words, the alias won't get substituted before attempting completion.

# Expansion

The shell allows you to perform different types of manipulations right before executing a line. In the following section we'll learn how to take advantage of each of the different forms of expansion and substitution available in zsh.

# Parameter expansion

Parameter expansion allows you to replace known variables in between the assignments of the command line. Simply put, parameter substitution is the mechanism by which the shell can change the following:

```
% foo=Hello
```

It will be changed to the following:

```
% echo "${foo}, world!"
> Hello, world!
```

Notice how the variable `foo` we declared in the previous line is replaced inside the arguments of `echo` with its actual value. You should be paying special attention to that peculiar `${}` construction. What happens is that when zsh reads the `${foo}` construction, it immediately knows it has to replace what's in it with whatever value it holds.

The astute reader might also have taken notice of the double quotes that surround the `echo` arguments. It's important to remember that just like aliases and prompt sequences, parameter substitution will work for arguments passed between double quotes, just like every other variable out there.

# Command substitution

Like parameter expansion, command substitution allows the shell to execute a command call and replace its output within a specially formed syntax. Command substitution usually takes the form of `` `command` ``, a program name wrapped around back quotes.

There's another form of program substitution available in newer shells such as zsh, which takes the form of `$(command)`. Both forms of substitution, `` `` `` and `$()`, mean the same; however, back quotes are considered a bit more portable, as they are recognized on pretty much every other shell out there.

In the wild, command substitution is frequently used to find out the full path to a command:

```
% print $(which zsh)
/usr/local/bin/zsh
```

Or, to make it more portable:

```
% print `which zsh`
/usr/local/bin/zsh
```

# Arithmetic expansion

Don't let the name discourage you; just like parameter substitution, arithmetic expansion is yet another form of substitution to help us sail swiftly across the command line. As its name implies, you can expand your input into a series of elements that will otherwise require you to type a lot.

Let's try it:

```
% echo $(( 5 + 4 ))
> 9
```

We started with some rather simple arithmetic expression (I know, I know; Math). But fret not, what just happened can be easily explained. We already know `echo` prints information into the standard output, so there are no mysteries there. What follows it is just an arithmetic expression using the $(( )) construct. Notice that, unlike parameter substitution, this kind of arithmetic substitution requires an extra set of parentheses. This is our way of letting zsh know that it needs to work with numbers, and that's why our 5 + 4 is treated as such.

The same rules apply to the following:

```
% echo $(( 5 + 4 * 3 ))
> 17
```

Which leads us to realize we need more parentheses for operator precedence:

```
% echo $(( (5 + 4) * 3 ))
> 27
```

Remember, the $(( )) construct is just a special construct, it's what tells zsh to treat what resides inside as arithmetic expressions.

Interestingly, we can invite parameter substitution to this party too. Looks like variables can also be substituted inside arithmetic expressions:

```
% num=5+4
% echo $(( num * 3 ))
> 27
```

In the preceding snippet, we declare a variable to hold our 5 + 4 expression; this makes num a container that, when asked what's up, will yell out our 5 + 4 expression. An easy way to check this is:

```
% echo ${num}
> 5+4
```

Note however, that by using num in the expression we did not require an extra set of parentheses in order to set operator precedence. This is because our num variable gets replaced on the following line with its value, which leaves us with an expression equivalent to (5 + 4) * 3. Expressions get evaluated before they are replaced, otherwise the result of the preceding call would have been 17.

Let's kick it up a notch with another handy arithmetic substitution:

```
% num=5+
% echo $(( $num 4 ))
> 9
```

On this opportunity, we are leaving the num expression as something that resembles "add whatever follows to it". This is why when it is evaluated on the next line, it gets replaced for what you'd expect, in this case 5 +. See that $ right before the num variable? Remember parameter substitution from the beginning of this section? That's what's going on here. Without that $num there, zsh simply does not know how to deal with the num assignment:

```
# This is horribly wrong!
% num=5+
% echo $(( num 4 ))
> zsh: bad math expression: operator expected at `4 '
```

Remember, if you wish to substitute a parameter, use $:

```
% echo $(( $num 4 ))
```

 You can always have a look at all supported types of expansions by typing man zshexpn on your console.

# Brace expansion

Another useful type of expansion is known as brace expansion. As the name implies, its syntax has to do with the use of curly braces ({ })—I suppose "curly brace expansion" was a bit too verbose when they were picking a name for it. Brace expansion allows you to declare an array of entries as follows:

```
% echo picture.jp{eg,g}
> picture.jpeg picture.jpg
```

What happens then is that the {eg,g} construct gets expanded into an array containing the elements eg and g. The shell then loops through those elements, passing two arguments to the echo command, which basically has the same meaning as typing the following:

```
% echo picture.jpeg
% echo picture.jpg
```

But you saved yourself from quite a few keystrokes and the accompanying boredom. Let's try another example:

```
% touch log_00{1,2,3}.txt
% ls
> log_001.txt  log_002.txt  log_003.txt
```

This time we are creating simple logfiles with the pattern log_00<num>.txt. The shell expands the {1,2,3} element into the elements 1, 2, and 3, and then calls the touch command three times:

```
% touch log_001.txt
% touch log_002.txt
% touch log_003.txt
```

In case you didn't notice, we use commas (,) in order to declare each of the elements inside curly braces. Now, you might be thinking "what happens when we use a longer array?" Here's when it gets even more interesting; declare a range of values:

```
% touch log_{007..011}.nfo
% ls | grep .nfo
log_007.nfo  log_008.nfo [...] log_010.nfo  log_011.nfo
```

It's worth noting a couple of things going on with the preceding example. I took the liberty to format the output of the list. But that (...) implies files 007 to 011 do exist. Firstly, we are now using brace expansion to extend a range, this time from nine up to eleven. The next thing that's also worth mentioning is that zsh is smart enough to notice the leading zeros and use it as a padding for the other values instead of replacing them with, say, vanilla integers. That is why you see the sequence starting with log_007.nfo and ending with log_011.nfo.

On the second line, we use a pipe symbol (|) to link or redirect output between different commands on your shell. This way we are listing the contents of the file, and redirecting the output into the utility grep, so we can filter said output by the .nfo extension.

Arrays can get even more interesting when we sparkle a bit more math in them:

```
% foo=(A B C)
% bar=(1 2 3)
% echo $^foo-$^bar
> A-1 A-2 A-3 B-1 B-2 B-3 C-1 C-2 C-3
```

In the preceding snippet, we declare two arrays, one containing the elements A, B, and C, and the other with the elements 1, 2, and 3. The call to echo then passes the argument ${^foo}-${^bar}. Notice the ^ operator (curly braces were implicit on the previous call, so I added them here for the sake of clarity). Again, we are telling zsh to expand the variables that come after the $ character, only this time we get a **Cartesian product** instead of, say, A B C-1 2 3. This is because the ^ operator serves as the array expansion expression. So as far as zsh is concerned, we're using each element of the array independently.

For a more detailed description of how array expansion and the ^ operator works, visit man zshoptions (particularly, the RC_EXPAND_PARAM section) and man zshexpn.

As with other sequences, some characters are considered "special" and need to be escaped. Commas and single quotes need to be escaped with a backslash:

```
% echo \'{\,,\'}\'' needs to be escaped'
> ',' needs to be escaped ''' needs to be escaped
```

# Working with history

Like an elephant, many modern Unix shells tend to remember in great detail the copious amount of commands entered while working with them. As many others, zsh too boasts a history log and an even more convenient way of accessing each of its entries. Being able to glimpse at what you have been up to is not only practical from a work-log perspective, but also as a way to speed things up. Think about it; you could use history to see (and eventually edit) a previously typed command, get a bit of context as to what's going on with your system, or avoid retyping the same thing over and over. Being able to easily retrieve a command from the past sounds awesome, because it is indeed a really neat feature.

We'll now take a look at how to use zsh's history expansion to work with previous entries in the command line.

**Working with history**

A more traditional approach to recalling history entries is by using the up arrow and down arrow keys on your keyboard to scroll through history entries. We'll have a closer look at how to alter this behavior when we examine the zsh line editor (ZLE) module in the next chapter. For now, we'll pretend that these are the only keys to move around history.

# History expansion

One of the ways zsh provides for you to access your history is via the so-called history expansion. This works whenever your input begins with the bang ! special character. As we saw in the previous chapter, the default behavior of the ! character can be overridden by setting the histchars shell parameter to something different:

```
% set histchars='@^#'
```

Unlike other shells though, zsh accepts up to three parameters when setting histchars. In addition to expansion (changed to @), the other two are used for substitution (^) and comments (#) respectively.

By replacing the default bang (!) with the @ character, you can now do things like calling your last executed command line as follows:

```
% ls *.txt
> readme.txt notes.txt
% @@
% ls *.txt
> readme.txt notes.txt
```

By redefining `histchars` you'll be able to use commands that actually require special characters such as ! without the need to escape them or worry about history substitution. You can choose any combination that you want, but, as a rule of thumb, try to stick with the less frequently used characters so that it is actually worth the effort.

 History expansion will only work if you are running an interactive shell and the option `NO_BANG_HIST` is unset in your `.zshrc` file.

Accessing your history entries is done via what we call *event designators*. Like escape sequences, designators are fancy names for constructs that the shell expands in order to know exactly what needs to be retrieved from history. One of the most popular and helpful event designators is the double bang (`!!`), which by itself refers to the most recent command entered:

```
% sh myscript.sh
> myscript.sh: Error: you need to be root to execute this.
% sudo !!
> myscript.sh: executing myscript.sh
```

As you can see, the `!!` character can be really useful for those occasions when you forget to run something on elevated privileges. What happens then is that zsh immediately expands the reference to the last command in history and replaces it in the line that contains the `sudo` call, saving you from entering the whole line again.

Having the shell making substitutions and automatically executing commands demands a bit more "blind faith" than most of us would like to deposit on their shell. Luckily, we can set the `HIST_VERIFY` option in `.zshrc` to force zsh into asking for confirmation every time you bang a command:

```
% setopt HIST_VERIFY
% echo 'Hello!'
> Hello!
% !!
% echo 'Hello!'
```

As you can see, the shell completes the input in your prompt using the previous command, but does not execute it. This is really useful for things like elevated privileges or sudo commands. Feel free to go ahead and add `setopt HIST_VERIFY` to your `.zshrc` file, as we'll assume it is being used from now on.

That's really neat for the command we just typed, but what if the previous command is further back in the history timeline? Well, then we need to use the vanilla event bang:

```
% !cat
% cat /etc/hosts | grep 127.0.1.1
```

Here my last executed command that had `cat` in it was a printout of my `hosts` file (`cat /etc/hosts`), followed by a call to `grep` as I was looking for lines that have `127.0.1.1` on them.

If you connect to a remote host using SSH, you could use something like the following to retrieve the last run connection:

```
% !ssh
% ssh gfestari@192.168.1.10
```

As you can see, the syntax for history expansion is fairly easy to remember. Just put a ! character together with the command you're looking for and let zsh work its magic.

> *Word designators* indicate the words of the command line that will be included in a history reference. What follows is a quick reference of the available designators:
>
> - `^`: The first argument.
> - `$`: The last argument.
> - `%`: The most recent match for a given word.
> - `x-y`: A range of words. Negative indexes like `-i` mean `0-i`; thus, `-1` would mean "the penultimate entry".
> - `*`: All the arguments. Return null for events with just one word.
>
> Note that a `%` word designator will only work when used as `!%`, `!:%`, or `!?str?:%`; anything else and you will be greeted with an error.
>
> For a more in-depth look at word designators and history expansion semantics, please refer to `man zshexpn`, particularly the section titled "HISTORY EXPANSION".

Let's kick it up a notch then; you can combine the special characters `^` and `$` in order to access the first and last arguments of a history entry respectively:

```
% mkdir new_folder
% cd !^
% cd new_folder
```

The ^ character gets expanded into the first argument of the mkdir command, which in this particular case is new folder.

```
% touch log1.txt log2.txt
% nano !$
% nano log2.txt
```

Here the same happens with $, only this time the last argument of the touch command is expanded so we can eventually edit it using nano.

If you are familiar with regular expressions, both of these designators' behavior shouldn't be too surprising. However, if what you need to do is access some string that is not located either at the beginning (^) or end ($) of the history, then you need the ? designator:

```
% !?etc
> cat /etc/hosts | grep 127.0.1.1
```

The preceding expression matches the most recent command containing etc. Generally speaking, the syntax for using the ? event designator can then be summed up as follows:

```
!?str[?]
```

The optional ? you see there at the end is only necessary if the command is followed by any text that is not to be considered part of str; for example:

```
% !?etc?^
> /etc/hosts
```

Did you notice how both the ? characters serve as delimiters for the etc keyword? Think of them as parentheses that wrap the expression you're trying to match. The caret operator (^) is there as we are interested in the first argument of that particular command line, which coincidentally is the /etc/hosts string.

There's lots more we can do with the history bang operator. Another neat trick is that it can refer to a particular line in your history. As before, the syntax is merely a tweak of what we already know:

```
!<hist_number>
% !103 # this retrieves the 103rd entry in your $HISTFILE.
% !4   # this retrieves the 4th entry.
```

But what about knowing which line I want to use? Well, that's a bit more complex, but not as much as using `grep`, `ack`, or whatever it is that kids are using these days to search within your history file:

```
% history | grep nano
> 2045  nano /etc/hosts
```

Using `grep` and searching for entries that feature `nano`, I can see that I edited `/etc/hosts` with it, and that the record resides on line `2045` of my `$HISTFILE`. If we wanted to open the hosts file again, it'll be a simple matter of calling:

```
% !2045
% nano /etc/hosts
```

And now for a bit of mix and match:

```
% history | grep git
> 1571  cd ../git/dotfiles
  1572  git status
  1573  git diff zsh/zsh_funcs
  1574  git diff zsh/zshrc
  1584  history | grep git
```

On this opportunity I'm looking for `git` entries. As you can see from the results, there are quite a few things I've been doing with it. Combine what we have learned so far, and we can accomplish quite a few things:

```
% more !1573$
% more zsh/zsh_funcs
```

As you can see, we used the bang operator together with the $ selector to refer to the last argument of line 1573 of our history.

Interestingly, you can also use a negative integer to refer to the nth-to-last entry:

```
% !-2 # this will retrieve the 2nd to last entry in history.
% !-97 # this does the same to the 97th to last entry.
```

Negative indexes should be pretty familiar territory for some programmers (I'm looking at you, Python and Ruby developers).

# History substitution

Another helpful feature of the history expansion on zsh is command substitution. Using this kind of substitution, you can avoid re-entering a whole line of your shell history just so you can edit a comparatively smaller section of it.

Raise your hand if you have made something like the following:

```
% ls
> dir1  file.txt
% mv fiel.txt dir1/
mv: rename fiel.txt to dir1/fiel.txt: No such file or directory
```

It seems I misspelled the `file.txt` name, so what now? Traditional history usage would suggest we just press the up arrow key to recall the previous line, navigate left to the `fiel` typo, re-type the correct name, and be done with it. The zsh approach however, is a bit more practical:

```
% ^fiel^file
% mv file.txt dir1/
```

What sorcery is this? Put simply, the chained ^ operator allows you to match the first occurrence of a word and replace it with the word attached to the second ^ operator. A more general syntax would be:

```
^history-entry^word-replacement
```

You can prevent a command from being added to your history by setting `HIST_IGNORE_SPACE` in your startup options. This will make the shell ignore the lines that start with a space.

```
% echo "this line will be recorded in history"
%  echo "this will not"
```

# More useful options

To round off this section, here are a couple of history-related options worth considering when populating your startup files, in addition to what we have already discussed throughout this chapter. Just put any (or all) of these on your `.zshrc` and remember to append `setopt` before each entry.

- `EXTENDED_HISTORY`: Saves a timestamp and duration for each history entry run. An excellent addition for the data analysis aficionado.

- `HIST_IGNORE_ALL_DUPS`: Ignores duplicate entries when showing results.

- `HIST_FIND_NO_DUPS`: Does not display eventual duplicates of a line that has already been found.

- `HIST_REDUCE_BLANKS`: Removes extra spaces and tabs from history entries.

- `INC_APPEND_HISTORY`: Adds entries to the history as they are typed, that is, doesn't wait until the shell exits. Probably one of the most awesome features of zsh. You know you want this.

- `SHARE_HISTORY`: Shares history between different zsh processes. Another great option to compliment the previous entry.

# Summary

In this chapter we had a look at some of the most prominent time-saving features of zsh. The purpose of this entry in our shell adventure was to start accomplishing more by typing less. Thus, this chapter focused on understanding aliases, how they work, and how to roll our own keystroke-saving definitions in a way that won't cause more trouble than what they attempt to solve.

We then moved onto expansions, learning the ways of arithmetic and brace expansion in order to make command-line related chores feel more like a breeze. Finally, we took a closer look at how to work with history, going beyond the keyboard arrow-mashing approach and learning history expansion and event designators in order to avoid repeating ourselves into oblivion.

By now you should have a fairly solid notion regarding the following:

- **Aliases**: We learned what an alias is and how to define a useful shortcut for our commands together with a handful of tips to start your collection.

- **Parameter expansion, command substitution, and arithmetic and brace expansion**: How to replace entries on the command line with the output of any given program, the result of an arithmetic expression, and even how to expand arrays so you don't have to type the same thing more than once.

- **History expansion and substitution**: How to apply all of the above, together with some more specific constructs such as the double bang (!!) to the shell's history and avoid repeating yourself to boredom.

Not bad at all. Pat yourself on the back or go grab a beer, by now you should feel confident enough to work your way around zsh without problems. That's great, but there's still much more left for us to discover, so don't slack! Next in store for us is ZLE, the zsh line editor. We'll get to know another of zsh's cooler features and discover that we don't actually require a dedicated program in order to perform some of the more advanced text processing on the command line. Besides saving us hundreds of hours of mind-numbing repeated keystrokes, we'll also learn how to customize the editor's shortcuts and key bindings so we don't have to rely on guesswork anymore.

# 3
# Advanced Editing

In this chapter, we are taking a step forward from basic zsh usage and diving into the more advanced features of the command line. We will be getting close and personal with the zsh line editor, understanding how it works and why zsh needs it's very own input editor. We will discover new ways of accessing and tapping into the shell's history and learn some new command line editing tricks in order to speed up most of our regular tasks and avoid repeating ourselves to boredom. Finally, we will discover that there's really no need to be limited to a single line of text while using zsh.

## Zsh line editor

In the previous chapter, we learned how to access the shell's history and how to use some special escape sequences in order to access its records. Nevertheless, we assumed that the only way for us to review previous history entries was by using the arrow-up and down keys on the keyboard and loop through them sequentially. Well, as you can imagine, it's time we got acquainted with another of zsh's great features: the zsh line editor.

Unlike other shells—I'm looking at you, Bash—zsh does not depend on GNU's `readline` library, rolling instead with its own version of a command line editor that boasts most of the bells and whistles you'd expect to find in a full-fledged application. The zsh line editor, or ZLE in short, allows you to define your own key bindings (a combination of key presses) and set of custom keymaps (collections of key bindings) in addition to extending predefined entries. ZLE is also a key module of zsh, and is present in any interactive shell you use. Luckily, zsh is smart enough to know when not to load ZLE, thus avoiding extra resources if ZLE is not required.

# Getting to know ZLE

By now, you have been using zsh long enough to notice that some things just seem odd; like when you press a key, say *PageUp*, you are bound to see some arcane glyphs, same as trying to use the *Ctrl* + left-arrow shortcut to move the cursor between words. As it stands, ZLE is the one in charge of knowing what these symbols mean and what behavior is linked to them, a task we need to set up via key bindings. We can even group our collection of keybinds under the same name and use different collections for altogether different purposes such as *Home* to move to the beginning of the line when editing commands or selecting the first entry when searching through history. But first, let's take advantage of what's already defined in a default installation of zsh and the vanilla ZLE.

# Working with keymaps

On its own, ZLE comes with some handy bindings in order to cater to Emacs and vi users, some of the most popular editors out there. ZLE supports both vi *insert* and *read* modes, but defaults to Emacs as this seems to be the most user-friendly mapping for new users.

You can access it at any time by typing `bindkey -e` in the command line. We will be using the Emacs keybinds throughout this book, but feel free to roll with the vi mode if you feel more comfortable with it. You can always go back to Emacs mode by typing `bindkey -e` into your terminal. Whatever you choose, keep in mind that ZLE works only in interactive shell sessions, and that you will need to add your different configuration entries and bindings to your `.zshrc` file as they will be needed to be set for each session.

> Zsh relies on your environment variables `$EDITOR` and `$VISUAL` in order to guess—make an educated guess, that is—which keybind it will default ZLE to. However, note that names such as `vile`, which contain the string `vi`, will trigger the use of vi keymap. You can add your own safety net of sorts, simply by adding `bindkey -e` in your `.zshrc` file to avoid possible conflicts and explicitly setting the layout.

For example, in order to default each new session to the Emacs mode, open up your `.zshrc` and append the following line:

```
bindkey -e
```

Having a default set in your startup files does not mean you have to commit to it at all times though. You can switch between vi and Emacs modes respectively, simply by typing the following line:

```
% bindkey -e
```

or

```
% bindkey -v
```

By using the e or v options, you are telling bindkey to link the provided emacs or viins keymaps to the main alias, which in turn gets loaded by default during startup. If anything goes awry, ZLE will default to .safe, which is a very constrained mode that provides you with the bare essentials. In such cases, your best shot at jumping out of the frying pan is by typing things such as bindkey -e and pressing *return* in order to switch keybinds. As you might expect then, using .safe spells trouble with your configuration and thus, is a binding you really don't want to see that often.

> As vi users might expect, zsh provides two keymaps for vi: viins and vicmd. Be careful when tinkering with those though, as defaulting to vicmd will leave you without the ability to insert any kind of text.

# Basic editing

Now that we have set our default key mapping to Emacs, we can start discussing some of its more interesting features such as keyboard shortcuts that speed up your tasks.

The following table contains some useful Emacs mappings:

| | |
|---|---|
| *Ctrl + A* | Moves the cursor to the beginning of the line |
| *Ctrl + E* | Moves the cursor to the end of the line |
| *Ctrl + W* | Deletes the whole word backwards from the cursor location |
| *Esc + B* | Moves the cursor backwards one word |
| *Esc + F* | Moves the cursor forward one word |
| *Ctrl + D* | Deletes a character (moves forward) / lists completions / logs out |
| *Ctrl + U* | Deletes the whole line |
| *Ctrl + K* | Kills (or deletes) until the end of the line |

| | |
|---|---|
| *Esc + D* | Deletes one word on the right of the cursor |
| *Esc + Backspace* | Deletes one word on the left of the cursor |
| *Ctrl + Y* | Yanks the last killed word |
| *Esc + Y* | Switches the last yanked word |
| *Ctrl + T* | Transposes two characters |
| *Esc + T* | Transposes two words |
| *Ctrl + R* | Incremental search backwards |
| *Ctrl + S* | Incremental search forwards (automatically enables NO_FLOW_CONTROL option) |

*Depending on your keyboard and input configuration, you could replace the Esc + button sequences with what is commonly known as the Meta key. This is usually mapped to the Alt key; however, we'll refer to these kinds of mappings with the Esc + sequences throughout this text, since they sport the same behavior and are arguably more portable.*

## Going back and forth with words

The *Esc + B* and *Esc + F* bindings are tightly related to the WORDCHARS shell variable. This is zsh's way of knowing where any given word begins, although the definition of "word" might be rather peculiar for those coming from other shells. Particularly, the WORDCHARS shell variable defaults to… well, see it for yourself:

```
% echo $WORDCHARS
> *?_-.[]~=/&;!#$%^(){}<>
```

See those symbols? These are also considered as part of any given word (besides alphanumeric characters, that is). What's important to keep in mind here is the rather bipolar behavior of the shell; a character is either part of a word, or it isn't. Keep this in mind when using sequences such as *Esc + B* or *Esc + F*, and remember you can always override the WORDCHARS definition in those rare occasions where it might be required.

## Yanking and transposing text

You might have noticed the terms *yanking* and *transposing* in the shortcuts table and immediately addressed your thoughts with a healthy dose of what? So let's expand a bit more on that.

Transposing (*Ctrl + T*) might be a fancy name, but rest assured its functionality is nowhere near as complicated to understand as it sounds. Put simply, transposing a character will swap its place with the one immediately following it on the right, making it march valiantly towards the end of the line, one place at a time. Once there, it'll only swap positions with the character immediately before it. This might be a bit confusing, so let's get going with an example as follows:

```
% echo bca

> bca
```

That's not right. Let's edit our previous history entry:

```
% echo bca
```

Now move your prompt on top of a—the more straightforward way of doing this is by hitting the end-of-the line shortcut, *Ctrl + E*—and hit the transpose shortcut, *Ctrl + T*.

```
% echo bac
```

a and c switched places. Progress! Now go back one char to the left, placing your cursor on top of a again and, again hit the transpose shortcut.

```
% echo abc
```

Success! As we'll see in *Chapter 5, Completion*, automatic completion will amend most of these silly mistakes; however, transposing comes in really handy on those occasions when you mistype things like parameter flags or URLs.

```
% git psuh origin master
```

A mistyped `git push` sentence can be easily fixed by simply navigating to u in psuh and hitting transpose.

```
% git push origin master
```

The same rules apply to the word transposing mechanism (*Esc + T*). The only difference, as you might have guessed already, is that it works with whole words instead of just chars.

As the old saying goes, actions speak louder than words, so the following is another example, this time by transposing words:

```
% echo 'world hello,'
```

Whoops! Got that completely backwards, time for some *Esc + T*. Put your prompt's cursor right on top of hello and hit the transpose shortcut.

```
% echo 'hello, world'
```

Sure enough, this will give the *Backspace* key a much-deserved vacation.

Yanking seems a bit harder to explain, but basically boils down to inserting a word you previously deleted by any of the kill shortcuts (*Ctrl + W, Ctrl + U, Ctrl + K, Esc + D, Esc + Backspace*). It works as follows:

Start typing your command.

```
% echo world hello
```

Realize you made a mistake, and kill the offending part. In this example, we use *Esc + Backspace* to delete the `hello` string.

```
% echo world _
```

Now move the cursor one word backwards, using the *Esc + B* bind.

```
% echo _world
```

And yank the `hello` string into the line by pressing *Ctrl + Y* (note that in this particular case, you will need to add an extra space between both the words and the _ character is there to show where the prompt cursor should be).

```
% echo hello_world
```

After using the *Ctrl + Y* shortcut for yanking, you can call the *Esc + Y* shortcut to swap between previously deleted words. The shell you see retains up to 10 deleted words in memory, in case you need to use them again. This sort of "deleted words clipboard" is popularly known as the kill ring due to its behavior—you will swap each of the killed words up to the last, and then start again from the very first by repeatedly pressing *Esc + Y*. However, note that pressing *Ctrl + Y* again will only insert a new previously yanked word.

# Revisiting history

As you might have noticed in the Emacs shortcuts table, there are quite a few shortcuts we can use to work with history. So let's put ZLE to better use and build on the *History expansion* section from *Chapter 2, Alias and History*, with our newly learned bindings.

Turns out we can use *Esc + <* to go to the very beginning of our history file, that is, the first entry of our log. Likewise, pressing *Esc + >* will deliver us to the end of the history file. However, that's hardly convenient for larger history logs. What we really need is to perform an incremental search. *Ctrl + R* is the default provided mechanism in zsh, and this will show us a prompt in which we can type to use as an immediate search filter. The more you type, the more precise the match is.

```
% # press Ctrl + R
bck-i-search: _
```

Start typing and once you have found the history entry you were looking for, you can either go ahead and press *return* to execute it, or the left-arrow/right-arrow key to edit the selected entry. You can exit this mode at any time by pressing *Ctrl + G*.

>  The incremental search mode has its own keymap, conveniently called `isearch`.

It's very likely that your terminal is set to use the *Ctrl + Q* and *Ctrl + S* combinations for flow control, respectively stopping and resuming any output to the terminal. In order to avoid overlapping the default `history-search-forward` binding (also *Ctrl + S*), zsh offers the `NO_FLOW_CONTROL` option, which can be set in your startup files.

```
setopt NO_FLOW_CONTROL
```

This will safely disable such behavior within the shell (other programs can depend on flow control normally) and thus, is the recommended way of using *Ctrl + S*.

# Advanced editing

So far we have discovered our way around the command line and started to get the hang of ZLE. It's time we kick it up a notch though, so we can see what the line editor is really capable of.

## ZLE-related options

This chapter wouldn't be complete without some options for us to tinker with now, would it? The following are some things to try if you are looking to modify ZLE's default behavior:

- `NO_BEEP`: This option skips beeping on errors.

- OVERSTRIKE: This defaults the editor to the insert mode. The way it works is that each new character replaces the one to the immediate right, instead of displacing it one position to the right as default.

- SINGLELINEZLE: It turns off multiline editing. No, I'm not on drugs. This could be used as a reminder of darker times.

Sprinkle some of these on your startup files (namely, .zshrc) and you'll be all set.

# Defining your own keymaps

Besides the Emacs and vi mode-setting options, the bindkey built-in allows you to create your own keymaps and alias them by using a couple of simple options. Namely, the -N flag will let you define a new keymap on the fly.

```
% bindkey -N newmap # this creates a keybind named 'newmap'
```

Or even create one based on an existing one.

```
% bindkey -N mycoolmap emacs # this creates a new keymap based off
  the existing 'emacs'
```

You can then alias your new keymap with the -A option by simply issuing the following command:

```
% bindkey -A mycoolmap mymacs # this creates an alias 'mymacs' for
  'mycoolmap'
```

Creating the alias mymacs for the existing mycoolmap keybind will allow you to eventually use bindkey -D mycoolmap to delete it without the fear of losing your settings. Turns out that both aliases are treated as separate keybinds; thus, deleting one does not affect the other. This proves useful during the time you are experimenting with bindings and wish to start from scratch, or just wish to have a backup of sorts for when things go awry. Be careful when naming your aliases though, as any existing keybind will be immediately replaced by the new alias if their names are the same!

You should avoid naming your own keymaps starting with the dot . character as future editions of zsh might eventually ship with conflicting namespaces.

The `bindkey` command also has quite a few other options at its disposal. Of particular interest when populating your startup files are the listing options. Namely, `l` and `L` allow you to list the available keymaps in different formats. By typing `bindkey -l`, you can quickly have a look at the currently available keymaps, while issuing `bindkey -lL` will format the output as a series of the `bindkey` commands.

```
% bindkey -lL
> bindkey -N command
  bindkey -N emacs
  bindkey -N isearch
  bindkey -N listscroll
  bindkey -A emacs main
  bindkey -N menuselect
  bindkey -N vicmd
  bindkey -N viins
```

You can also use this option in order to check if a particular keymap is a link:

```
% bindkey -lL mymacs
> bindkey -A mycoolmap mymacs
```

This tells you that, as expected, `mymacs` is an alias for the `mycoolmap` keymap we defined earlier on. By using the `-lL` option to check the `main` alias, you have a practical way of determining the keymap currently in use.

```
% bindkey -lL main
> bindkey -A emacs main
```

Finally, you can use the `-L` option to have a list of all your current bindings, including those of a built-in keymap, formatted in a way you can use within your scripts:

```
% bindkey -L
  bindkey "^@" set-mark-command
  bindkey "^A" beginning-of-line
  bindkey "^B" backward-char
  bindkey "^D" delete-char-or-list
  bindkey "^E" end-of-line
  bindkey "^F" forward-char
  bindkey "^G" send-break
  bindkey "^H" backward-delete-char
  # [...] large list of bindings omitted
  bindkey -R "\M-^@"-"\M-^?" self-insert
```

Just copy and paste the output into your startup files and you have the foundation for your custom keymap. It's just a matter of replacing the action or shortcut keys with something that better suits your needs, and you are done. Handy, isn't it?

> You can use the `read` utility in order to figure out the actual escape sequence your terminal emulator is sending to the shell; just call `read` and then input the sequence you want to try out. For example, the following is what *Ctrl + back-arrow* is sending on my system:
>
> ```
> % read
> > ^[[1;5D
> ```
>
> Some keys such as *Backspace* might require you to use the `-k` option, which allows you to specify the number of characters to read. Used by itself, it'll default to one.
>
> ```
> % read -k
> ```
>
> Now (press *Backspace*.)
>
> ```
> ^?
> % # and you are back to the prompt
> ```
>
> Keep in mind that you can exit the `read` command at any time by pressing *Ctrl + C*.

Emacs users will find themselves at home with the *Esc + X* sequence. By pressing *Esc* followed by the key *X*, ZLE greets you with an `execute` prompt. You can then start typing in your commands and even use the *Tab* key for auto-completion help. For example:

```
# type in "hello" and navigate to the beginning of the line (Ctrl + A)
followed by Esc + X
% _hello
execute:
# ZLE waits for your command, type `ca` and press Tab key:
% _hello
execute: ca

% _hello
execute: capitalize-word
# now press return and watch how the command is applied

% Hello
```

The reason we used *Ctrl + A* is for the prompt to be at the beginning of the line, just before the rest of the string.

 Remember that you can exit the execute prompt at any time by using the *Ctrl + G* sequence.

As the astute reader might have noticed, there are quite a few ways of achieving the same behavior, but that's partially missing the point of the execute sequence. It is there simply to allow you to do things you would normally not do (either because of an awkward shortcut or lack of muscle memory); execute it and its completion mechanism will make recalling commands a snap.

In the same vein as execute, where-is — which is unbound to any sequence by default — will show you how to perform any given command. Just call execute, type where-is (you can use Tab for completion just as before) and press *return*. This time you will be greeted with the Where is: prompt, where you can also use completion to list any command you are after. Press *return* for ZLE to show you the sequence bound to the said command. For example, we can use where-is to find an alternative shortcut to our capitalize-word example as follows:

```
% # enter where-is mode via Esc + X
> Where is: capitalize-word
> capitalize-word is on "^[C" "^[c"
```

Well, look at that. Turns out we can capitalize the word immediately after the prompt by using the *Esc + C* combination.

# Don't call them widgets

There comes a time in the life of any eager zsh learner to talk about widgets. It's time you and me had that talk already.

Ever wondered how all those keybindings and special actions are put together and work marvelously? Well, we have widgets to thank for that. See, zsh likes to delegate responsibilities whenever it can, and widgets are a prime example of that; instead of having to deal with handling every little action performed by key sequences (similar to those defined in your keymaps), zsh relies on widgets to do the actual work. Think of them as small functions designed to carry out a simple mission. I, on the other hand, like to think of them as those sneaky gnomes that make magic happen in the kitchen whenever I'm not around.

ZLE comes with quite a few built-in widgets, each boasting two names, a vanilla name and a hidden name, which is simply defined as the normal name and preceded by a dot . character. Hidden names are there just to signal that they can't be rebound to a different widget (thus creating a backup copy that's always available in case your keybind definitions go awry).

As you might have guessed, that's not the whole deal; widgets can be user-defined or defined by other modules (such as ZLE or the built-in FTP client, zftp).

# Defining your own widgets

Defining your own widgets doesn't get more complicated than calling zle -N with your widget's name on it.

```
autoload -Uz tetris
zle -N tetris
bindkey '\et' tetris
```

The previous example, a slight variation from one of the suggestions available at the zsh wiki site (http://zshwiki.org), binds the *Esc + T* combination to the built-in tetris module, so you can spend those idle times on the command line a bit more entertained.

Let's go over it, line by line:

```
autoload -Uz tetris
```

This is the good old autoload module, which handles the loading of different modules and functions across the shell. In this particular case, we're importing the tetris module for later use.

```
zle -N tetris
```

This is where the magic actually happens; we're defining the new widget by calling ZLE with the -N option and telling it that the name for our new widget is tetris.

 Keep in mind that hidden names are special for widgets, so refrain from using names starting with a dot ( . ).

We wrap up the definition simply by binding our newly defined widget to the *Esc + T* shortcut on the keyboard:

```
bindkey '\et' tetris
```

Notice that the bold **tetris** call there refers to the widget we defined and not the actual `tetris` module.

Now, to actually see this in action, you'll have to either add it to your `.zshrc` file or save it as a separate file and source it from `.zshrc`, just as we've done before. So go ahead and save this as `.zsh_tetris` in your `$HOME` folder, and source it from `.zshrc` by adding the following line:

```
source .zsh_tetris
```

Now go ahead and type *Esc + T* to enjoy your new widget.

Just some Tetris. Yes, I'm rusty.

## Special variables

Some special variables that are available in ZLE should come in handy when defining your own widgets for editing and/or manipulating the command line.

The following list contains some of the most commonly used references:

- CURSOR: This is the current position of the cursor on the command line.
- BUFFER: This contains the current editing buffer and can span multiple lines.

- LBUFFER/RBUFFER: These are the contents to the left and right of the current cursor, respectively. They too can span multiple lines.

- PREBUFFER: This contains the buffer already read when editing a continuation line.

- WIDGET: This gives the name of the widget currently in use by the editor.

By using these variables you can, for example, know precisely which character is currently under the cursor by simply using the ${BUFFER[CURSOR]} expression. This might as well read as "the value of the BUFFER array for the CURSOR position" (remember, CURSOR is just a number that tells which column the prompt is at).

# Your first function

You can achieve even more complex behavior by defining your own functions. Each time the widget is executed, it'll call the corresponding function. Let's kick it up a notch with our second widget.

For the following example, we'll work with a variant of the excellent rationalize-dot widget, as presented on the ZSH-LOVERS' manpage (http://grml.org/zsh/zsh-lovers.html):

```
function rationalize-dot {
  if [[ $LBUFFER = *.. ]]; then
    LBUFFER+=/..
  else
    LBUFFER+=.
  fi
}
zle -N rationalize-dot
bindkey . rationalize-dot
```

And now let's go ahead and go over it line by line.

Firstly, we're defining our own function here, called rationalize-dot. The way we declare a function is simply a matter of giving it a special name, followed by parentheses as follows:

```
my_function() {
    my_code
}
```

The curly braces {} you see there are the delimiters of the function body; whatever lays between them is considered part of the function, just like the my_code stub in the preceding example.

Alternatively, you can also define functions using the reserved keyword `function` and using a slight variation of the previous syntax as follows:

```
function my_function {
    my_code
}
```

As you can see, we trade the parentheses for the preceding function keyword. Otherwise, both syntaxes represent the same thing and are interchangeable. So pick whatever floats your boat.

Likewise, calling a function doesn't get any more complicated than explicitly writing its name; `my_function`, in this particular case.

Back to the `rationalize-dot` example, the second line there is an `if` statement, the most basic control flow mechanism provided by the shell. When used in its full glory, an `if` statement will resemble the following:

```
if condition; then
    my_code
elif another_condition; then
    more_code
else
    even_more_code
fi
```

In its most basic form, `if` statements test for a Boolean condition, an expression or command that resolves as either true or false (or has an exit status to indicate this), and takes action accordingly. Whatever is not suitable for the first clause, the `else` part will gladly take care of as follows:

```
if condition; then
    do_a_barrel_roll
else
    echo "can't do it"
fi
```

 Notice the `fi` at the end? Think of the first `if` as an opening brace { character, and the `fi` as the closing one }.

The previous sample will test the condition `condition`, if it evaluates to something that is true, our mock function will call the `do_a_barrel_roll` code. If `condition` is not true (what is popularly known as false), then the `else` block gets called, and dutifully issues an `echo "can't do it"` command.

The `elif` statement simply means "else, if" and is used to evaluate further conditions. You can add as many `elif` clauses as the options you have, but be careful when traversing down that road; neat code becomes wild spaghetti in a matter of keystrokes if not properly tamed.

In the `rationalize-dot` example, the `if` statement tests whether the `LBUFFER` variable matches the expression `*..`, which actually means "has the user typed anything followed by two periods?". If that's the case, then append a `/..` expression to the buffer variable. Otherwise, just let the `else` statement handle it.

As per the `else` block, it'll just add an actual period to the buffer:

```
else
    LBUFFER+=.
fi
```

This might not seem a logical decision at first, until we move into the following lines:

```
zle -N rationalize-dot
bindkey . rationalize-dot
```

The first one is the standard widget declaration we've seen before, but the binding immediately after it is what makes the `rationalize-dot` function require the `else` statement to add a period. As it's called on each dot press (the keybinding it's being assigned), this requires you to behave as an actual period key if the user hasn't typed anything yet.

As before, you can go ahead and add this to your `.zshrc` (or any other module that gets sourced by it) and take it out for a spin; just type `...` and see what happens after that third dot gets pressed.

As we'll see later in *Chapter 5, Completion*, you can also let the shell source functions automatically by extending or adding them to your `$fpath` variable.

This is particularly useful in combination with the `cd` command and an unhealthy dose of nested folders.

Want to go further? You'll find tons of predefined built-in widgets for customizing your keybindings in the `zshzle(1)` manpage's *STANDARD WIDGETS* section. Just type `man zshzle` to get started.

# Working with regions

Continuing the legacy of Emacs' inherited behavior, you can set regions in the command line by holding *Ctrl* and pressing the Space bar. This will trigger a region selection mechanism that you can expand with the arrow keys, which works just as if you were clicking and dragging your mouse to highlight text.

So, why bother with regions? You could, for example, mark a region via the *Ctrl* + Space bar sequence and then perform a command on top of it (similar to `capitalize-word` we saw earlier), or even mix-in the previously mentioned `execute-command` to call a function that has no keybind. Overall, these few niceties straight from Emacs give ZLE (and of course, zsh) the versatility to behave almost like a full-fledged editor.

# Multiline editing

At this point, it should be no surprise to learn that zsh is smart enough to notice when you aren't done with a line. Unlike most other shells though, zsh is also capable of suggesting what might be missing, or even allowing you to use multiple rows of lines for entering your commands. Unlike traditional continuation where you put a \ character at the end of the line and press *return* to continue on the one immediately below, ZLE will greet you with the $PS2 prompt and add more of context information.

On most flavors of Bourne-derived shells, you can use the following line:

```
% ls \
```

Press *return* (notice there is absolutely nothing after the \ char).

```
> -a
```

Press *return* again, and it'll work just like the `ls -a` command. Zsh will give you a bit more context as follows:

```
% echo " # press return immediately after the double quotes
dquote> _
```

The $PS2 prompt (the alternative/second prompt) is called in order to signal that the shell is waiting for the rest of the double-quote assignment. Go ahead and wrap it up as follows:

```
dquote> $HOME" # press return here
> /home/gfestari
```

There's more to multiline editing than alternative prompts though. You can use the *Esc + return* shortcut to add a new continuation line:

```
% echo hello world # press Esc + return
echo goodbye world
```

And press *return* to see both the lines execute sequentially, just as though it were a script. Keep in mind that you are not limited to just two lines and can add as many lines as you want.

This sorcery owes its powers to the `self-insert-unmeta` command, whose job consists simply of inserting a carriage return character into the line. So now you know that each time you press *Esc + return*, you are actually using a shortcut to the `self-insert-unmeta` command.

Besides the obvious "being different" feeling, what's really convenient about the *Esc + return* method is that you can move across lines as you please by using the arrow keys. To top it off, each multiline entry is treated as a whole line. Just press the up-arrow and you will see the block you previously typed come back to life for you to edit. While we are at it, I'd like you to meet the `push-line-or-edit` command, which allows you to convert a previously typed block of lines into a single block whenever you are on a continuation (otherwise it'll behave like a normal push-line command). It works more or less as follows:

Start entering your function in the command line, pressing *return* after the first `if` line:

```
% if [[ true = false ]]; then # press return here

then> echo _
```

And stop right there. Realize you have made a terrible mistake with the condition clause of the `if` statement (apart from the extremely simple logic... but hey, this is an example). Unfortunately, you can't scroll back to the previous line with the up-arrow button as you have already pressed *return* and that would trigger the history search behavior, so what's next? Well, `push-line-or-edit`, of course. Hit *Esc + X* in order to execute a command, and type `push-line-or-edit` (you can use the *Tab* key for completion) and press *return*.

The prompt will change to a traditional one (ditching the `then>` indicator from the continuation line), and you will have a new buffer filled with all your previously typed lines which, of course, you can edit at will as follows:

```
% if [[ true = false ]]; then
echo_
```

Seeing how much better a push-line `push-line-or-edit` is, it's of course advisable to bind it to the default `push-line` shortcut, either ^q or \eq:

```
bindkey '^Q' push-line-or-edit
bindkey '\eQ' push-line-or-edit
```

And now you can either use the *Ctrl + Q* or *Esc + Q* shortcuts to edit a whole block as if it were a single line. As with the `history-search-forward` binding we saw earlier (which defaulted to *Ctrl + S*), *Ctrl + Q* will require the `NO_FLOW_CONTROL` option to be set so as not to conflict with the terminal driver's behavior.

This whole thing started with `push-line-or-edit`, so it seems fair we got to discuss the actual `push-line` bit. This will be the default behavior when you are not on a continuation line. Just type your commands as usual, but do not press *return*:

```
% ls -a
```

Realize you are in the wrong directory, call our newly bound `push-line-or-edit` command via *Ctrl + Q*, and the prompt will be cleared for you as follows:

```
# push-line-or-edit
% _
```

Now use `cd` to go to the folder you were trying to list, and watch the buffer come back to life:

```
% cd myfolder
myfolder % ls -a
```

As soon as you execute a line, the prompt gets populated with the line you were editing prior to calling `push-line`.

# Putting it all together

As we saw earlier, a peculiar aspect of ZLE is that it has access to the shell's history, which of course means we can use some of the niceties we have learned in order to further improve how we work with it.

A neat way of taking advantage of the up/down arrow keys is via the `history-beginning-search` commands. We could define our own mappings in order to add some extra kick to the default behavior as follows:

```
bindkey '\e[A' history-beginning-search-backward
bindkey '\e[B' history-beginning-search-forward
```

Note that the \e escape sequence could also be replaced by ^[, thus leaving the bindings as ^[[A and ^[[B respectively.

Now, if you have an empty prompt and press the up-arrow key, it'll work by retrieving the most recent entry in the history as usual. However, as soon as you type something and press the up arrow key, it'll autocomplete with your most recent entry that matches with what's typed.

As an example, type the following pressing *return* after each line:

```
% echo hello world
% ls
% echo bye world
```

Now go ahead and press the up-arrow key. The natural backwards-scrolling sequence should be as follows:

```
> echo bye world
> ls
> echo hello world
```

Press *Ctrl + G* to exit the search mode. Now type ec and press the up arrow key:

```
% ec
> echo bye world
```

This comes in really handy during those times when you forget about a line mid-sentence and don't want to perform a search or discard the current line. Just remember to add your bindings into your startup files if you want to keep these kinds of changes between sessions!

# Summary

In this chapter we took a deep dive into what goes on between the prompt and the shell by the time you press *return*. We discovered some new tricks to work with history and tamed the default shortcuts by creating our own keymaps and bindings. As if this wasn't enough, you now know we are no longer limited to just working with one line, and that mistakes and distractions can easily be solved by a couple of keystrokes without us re-typing the whole line.

Okay, I'll admit it, we have been pretty busy in this chapter. So here's a chance to catch your breath while we go over everything we've covered in this sprint. What we have done is:

- Learned that zsh is made out of various modules, and got acquainted with ZLE

- Used key maps for editing text and learned about various shortcuts to improve our productivity in the command line

- Defined our own custom keymaps and worked with various regions and multiline prompts

- Learned about widgets, special functions that carry out every little task in the editor

- Written our first sample widgets to further extend the functionality of the editor and improve our shell experience

- Learned about functions and control flow via the `if` statements

- Finally, we learned that both modules and functions have special access to different parts of the shell, and we can do things such as hooking up ZLE widgets to keybindings in order to search the history.

Not a bad day I'd say. Now, let's head into the next chapter, where we'll learn about Globbing and filename generation, another of those features where zsh really shines. If you thought you had learned how to type less with ZLE in this chapter, wait until you see braces and qualifiers in action. Keep those elbows greased and that confidence up though, as there's still much more waiting for us to right around the corner.

# 4
# Globbing

In this chapter, we will get to know one of the most powerful features of zsh: filename generation. We will learn new ways of dealing with the system's files and directories and even expand the functionalities of some of the more traditional commands by applying parameter substitution and modifiers. The chapter also serves as an introduction to zmv, a built-in function that provides a number of useful functionalities to deal with both the mundane and the more complex tasks regarding files. We will learn to use zmv for renaming, copying, and linking files based on our newly learned patterns. Feeling excited already?

## Quoting your strings

A safe way of declaring your string variables involves the usage of quotes. Think of it as a way of telling the function "*here* starts and *over here* ends my string". Although not necessary on this particular example, you can quote a phrase when using echo as follows:

```
% echo 'this is a quoted phrase'
> this is a quoted phrase
```

Single quotes are treated as delimiters by the shell and as such, they are completely ignored. The same rule applies to the print built-in function:

```
% print 'this is a quoted phrase'
> this is a quoted phrase
```

So, what's the point of using quotes then? Well, imagine for a moment that your output looks something like the following:

```
% echo this is a backslash: \
~>
```

Yes, that will trigger a continuation line, so there's seemingly no way around it, save for using quotes. Let's try it again:

```
% echo 'this is a backslash: \'
> this is a backslash: \
```

So, as a rule of thumb, we use single quotes when there are special characters on our string as follows:

```
% echo 'special characters like * # and \ need to be quoted'
> special characters like * # and \ need to be quoted
```

Now, what's it that makes these special? Well, earlier in this book, we saw that comments are defined by a # sign; we can use the * character as a wildcard that matches filenames and the \ character can be used for escaping sequences with special meaning. Think of all these as *special characters* that will never literally mean what the keyboard says, unless you quote them.

> Some special characters need to be "escaped". This means that they will have a different meaning other than the characters they represent, unless there's a \ character before them, that is.

For example, echo *.rb will list all the files that have an .rb extension. If you wanted to list a directory named *.rb — weird, I know — you would have to call echo escaping the * special character as follows:

```
% echo \*.rb
```

Also worth noting is that \ is actually a special character, so in cases where a literal backslash is required, you will need to escape it too:

```
% echo \\
> \
```

As we saw in the previous chapter, a single backslash (\) will only trigger a continuation line.

You can make the shell output the raw string by supplying the (q) argument:

```
% string="This is a *string* with various 'special'
characters"
% echo ${(q)string}
> this\ is\ a\ \*string\*\ with\ various\ \'special\'\
characters
```

# Double quotes

Okay, so what happens when we need to use the niceties of the special characters and also need them to appear as their literal representations? Enter the double quotes.

The option RC_QUOTES allows you to use single quotes within a single-quoted string:

```
% setopt rcquotes
% echo 'a single ''quoted'' string'
> a single ''quoted'' string
```

Double quotes work by allowing you to retain the value of any string and also enabling *parameter substitution* and *shell expansion* within them.

Take a long, hard look at the following example:

```
% echo "My username is $(whoami) and my home folder is located at
'$HOME'."
> My username is gfestari and my home folder is located at '/Users/
gfestari'.
```

The shell works inside the double quotes by executing the command within the $() construct before anything else. In this particular case, we are using the whoami program to tell the current user ID—gfestari in this particular case—(if that's also your name, then *hello*, long-lost brother).

The shell then moves on to expand the environment variable $HOME, which holds the current user's home folder currently pointing at /Users/gfestari on my system. Notice how the single quotes are treated like any other character within double quotes.

# Getting started with Globbing

Filename Generation, popularly known as **Globbing** (as in, Global substitution), is the ability of the shell to generate filenames from patterns. This is but the name for the process that allows the shell to read a pattern and generate a series of filenames; as a matter of fact, you might notice you have been using Globbing for quite a while in this book, the only difference is, we're now formally introducing the feature. Also, be aware that whenever we mention *filenames* in this text, it means both file *and* folder names, as you can use pretty much the same patterns to match both.

The really important thing you need to remember when dealing with Globbing is that filename substitution happens in the shell *right before* the line you typed is sent to the command. In other words, you type, zsh does the substitution, and *only then* sends the result, an expanded string and not whatever you just typed, to the function or program. There are ways around this, but just be mindful.

If you'd like to take a deeper look at some of the features covered in this chapter, you can always refer to the official documentation by typing man zshexpn

# Globbing with the stars

Globbing works by using a series of special characters known as *operators*, to create a pattern that is later expanded by the shell into more complex, traditional strings without you even noticing the extra effort required. Arguably, the most popular of these operators is the asterisk or star (*). The star works as a *wildcard*, allowing you to match any filenames, even if you provide no pattern at all:

```
% echo *
README.md todo.txt draft.txt new_file.txt
```

This will list any file and folder on your current directory. Notice how we only needed a *single star* for this. However, if we want all files with a .txt extension, we simply need to provide the appropriate pattern: anything that ends with the desired extension.

```
% echo *.txt
todo.txt draft.txt new_file.txt
```

What happens is that zsh reads the *.txt pattern, transforms it into its literal meaning (all the filenames with a txt extension), and only then passes the result as the argument for echo, which in turn never deals with the actual pattern.

Arguably, the best thing the star has going on is its versatility. Just like a drunken sailor, a star can get along with practically anything, not just files:

```
% echo *folder
out_folder src_folder
```

You can use the NO_CASE_GLOB option if you want to make Globbing case-insensitive (that is, treat upper and lowercase characters as equals).

```
% setopt nocaseglob
% echo *.jpg
photo.jpg pic.JPG
```

It's not all sunshine and rainbows though. There's a fine print detail that you should consider when using the star operator: hidden files. If you recall from *Chapter 2, Alias and History*, we used an alias, la (or ls -a), in order to list the hidden files within a directory; otherwise, the command wouldn't list them.

Because of how big a headache it could cause you to do things like rm * and end up deleting a parent folder, most Unix shells will simply ignore hidden files for most commands. The same rules apply to Globbing when using the wildcard operator. A workaround for dealing with this behavior would be to explicitly use a pattern along the lines of .*some_pattern in order to include hidden files just like the following:

```
% echo .*zsh*
.zsh_aliases .zsh_funcs .zsh_history .zsh_prompt .zshenv .zshrc
```

We use two stars in order to list all the files that start with a dot (traditional hidden files in Unix) and contain a zsh pattern somewhere in their name. In other words, our startup files.

The takeaway lesson here: *you can use the star anywhere on a pattern*, you don't have to limit yourself with length or just extensions; be mindful of the hidden files though, as a star won't show you any hidden files, you'll need something along the lines of .*some_pattern for that to work.

You can always circumvent the "ignore files starting with dots" behavior by setting the GLOBDOTS option; however, it's advisable you refrain from setting it permanently on your startup files as it can lead to issues such as you deleting the parent (.) directory and so on.

The most important thing to keep in mind when using this option on your scripts or functions is ensuring a call to setopt NO_GLOBDOTS right before exiting. Most times though, you'll do just fine by using the .* pattern discussed previously.

# Questions for any single character

The question mark symbol works pretty much like the star, except it matches a single character instead of many. For example, you can use `ls ???` to list the contents of any three-lettered directory, or get a bit more practical and use the following to list any two-lettered extension file:

```
% echo *.??
script.sh
```

We can even view all files with an extension via the following, similar expression:

```
% echo main.?*
main.c main.o main.tmp
```

This is similar to the wildcard qualifier; however, you won't be able to match any filenames with leading dots unless you explicitly declare so.

# Brackets for a sequence of characters

You can use the square brackets construct to match a group of characters within a pattern. For example, you can use `[ML]*` to match any filename that starts with either an uppercase letter M or L.

```
% ls
Log.log Main.rb README.md script.sh
% echo [ML]*
Log.log Main.rb
```

Notice how we need to combine the character class operator with the wildcard in order to denote the filenames that might have more than a single uppercase letter.

Even more useful is the use of a hyphen (or minus sign) in order to name ranges of contiguous characters to match. For example, you can use the `[A-Z]*` pattern to match any file that starts with an uppercase letter from the alphabet. Likewise, you can use the same pattern for contiguous natural numbers:

```
% echo *.log_[1-9]
out.log_1 out.log_2 out.log_3
```

Simple enough, right? Remember you can declare your own character classes. Here's an example that matches any filename starting with any number from one to five or an uppercase M:

```
% echo [1-5M]*.*
Main.rb
```

Just as before, a [.]* pattern won't work as you might expect; in fact, it won't work at all.

**A note about ranges**

If your system is using a non-English alphabet or something other than the ASCII character set, chances are you might expect things like ü to match classes like [a-z]. This behavior, however, is ruled by the LANG and LC_* family of environment variables and is *very* system dependent, not to mention, beyond the scope of this book.

# Using safer ranges on your scripts

Although nothing to write home about if you have been using any modern shell lately, there's a series of shortcuts that save you from boredom when working with the garden variety of character classes. You can access them via the [[:shortcut:]] pattern.

So, for example, if you needed any letter from the alphabet (say, the range that includes both uppercase and lowercase English characters [A-Za-z]), you could use the alpha shortcut to list any filename that starts with a character from the alphabet like so:

```
% echo [[:alpha:]]*
```

Feeling enthusiastic about character sets already? The following table lists some of the popular ones:

| Character set | Description |
| --- | --- |
| ascii | Anything from the ASCII character set (see man ascii) |
| lower | Lowercase character |
| upper | Uppercase character |
| alpha | Letter |
| digit | Number |
| alnum | Alphanumeric character |
| print | Any printable character |
| blank | Space or tab character |
| space | Space character (tab, carriage return, newline and co.) |
| punct | Anything but an alnum nor a space |

You can combine multiple patterns and character sets; just remember that the innermost brackets belong to the character set, and everything else goes between the outermost brackets. For example, if we want all the files that start with either a `digit` character or the lowercase `b` letter, we might roll with the following:

```
% echo [[:digit:]b]*.c
bindings.c
```

As you can see, the inner set of brackets declares the character set, while the `b` character is there just as though we had typed `[b]`.

# Avoiding characters

Okay, we have been giving patterns a warm welcome so far, but what happens when we want the thing that does *not* match whatever we're looking for? Turns out there's also an easy way to tell zsh "I want the filenames that have nothing to do with this particular pattern", so let's get to it.

Suppose we have the following files in a given directory:

```
% ls
bindings.c  bindings.h  bindings.o  main.c  main.o
```

And we just want to select the actual code files, the ones ending in `.c` and `.h`, and avoid everything ending in `.o`. With what we have learned so far, we could get away with something along the lines of the following:

```
% echo *.[hc]
bindings.c bindings.h main.c
```

But as you can see, the more complex our requirements, the more likely we end up with a gigantic mess of a character class. Luckily, we can get the complement of a class via the caret (`^`) operator:

```
% echo *.[^o]
bindings.c bindings.h main.c
```

What we did back there was told zsh to expand the class for those filenames *that do not match* the o extension. Notice how the rest of the pattern remains unchanged and the caret is immediately after the left bracket that does the actual negation. Feel free to read this as "anything but whatever comes inside the brackets".

You can negate a character set by using a caret before the inner brackets. For example, if we wish to skip files that start with an uppercase letter, we might as well do the following:

```
% echo [^[:upper:]]*
```

# Handling mismatches

So far we have seen how to make the shell interpret our patterns and attempt to match whatever filenames it can. During the remainder of this Globbing trip of ours, we'll take a look at what happens with the unlucky patterns, those that fail to match anything and how the shell deals with them.

Let's try listing some nonexistent zip files:

```
% ls
bindings.c  bindings.h  bindings.o  main.c  main.o


% echo *.zip
zsh: no matches found: *.zip
```

It seems that zsh defaults to an error message and aborts the execution of the command. Luckily, there are plenty of things for us to do about it in the form of options.

First, there's NULL_GLOB, which will make the shell discard any pattern without a proper match. The following is an example, where a blank line gets printed when no matches are performed:

```
% setopt null_glob
% echo *.zip
>
```

This comes in handy when passing multiple patterns, but can make you call some programs without any arguments whatsoever, so consider that before updating your startup files willy-nilly.

```
% echo *.c *.zip
bindings.c main.c
```

The first pattern (*.c) matches and lists all files with a .c extension; whereas the second pattern (*.zip) doesn't match anything and is discarded (a null second entry is passed to echo).

Moving on, there's also the NOMATCH option, which you can unset to achieve a behavior that pretty much emulates bash; any pattern that does not match is passed as a *literal argument* to the command. This is relatively easy to test with the following example:

```
% unsetopt nomatch
% echo *.zip
*.zip
```

What do you know? Seems the manpage was right and now the failing *.zip pattern acts just as though we had called echo '*.zip'. This works differently from NULL_GLOB, in that the pattern is also ignored by the shell, but passed *as an argument* to the program regardless of it matching anything.

 Remember you could also use setopt NO_NOMATCH instead of unsetopt.

Lastly, there's an option which mimics the legacy behavior of csh, aptly named CSH_NULL_GLOB. Yes, naming conventions spare no expenses. Anyway, here's what happens when you set it:

```
% setopt csh_null_glob
% echo *.zip
zsh: no match
```

Seems it's back to the "error message and abort command" zone for us. Like the curious learners we are, let's kick it up a notch and see what happens when dealing with multiple patterns:

```
% echo *.c *.zip
bindings.c main.c
```

Ok, now that's a lot nicer. What happens is that CSH_NULL_GLOB will show you an error message and abort the command line whenever any single pattern does not match, but will go ahead and discard the failing patterns if there's at least one that matches. Think of this as the product of that night of unrestrained passion between zsh's default behavior and NULL_GLOB. And while we're at it, don't blame me for that mental picture.

Before we move on to another subject though, there's another option you should familiarize yourself with when dealing with patterns. But first, let's take a look at what happens when we try to pass a wrong pattern to the shell:

```
% echo *[[:alpha:]]
zsh: bad pattern: *[[:alpha:]]
```

Notice how we missed the closing bracket (]? The shell complains about the pattern and we are left with the sour taste of failed scripting. Let's try that again, but now we'll set the following option:

```
% setopt no_bad_pattern
% echo *[[:alpha:]
*[[:alpha:]
```

We turned on NO_BAD_PATTERN (or unset BAD_PATTERN, whatever floats your boat) and guess what happened? That's right; the bad pattern *is ignored* by the shell expansion mechanism and passed instead as an argument to the command. Pretty handy if you don't want those pesky warnings while experimenting with your newly learned patterns.

# Extended Globbing

As you might have noticed at this point, when it comes to Globbing, zsh goes above and beyond the call of duty and then some more. What we'll discuss next is the more advanced aspects of Globbing, commonly referred to as *extended Globbing*. Put simply, we'll learn a new set of characters and expressions that expand on what we have been using to provide even more functionality to the shell's operations. However, before we ride that horse, pry open that .zshrc file of yours and add the following option:

```
setopt EXTENDED_GLOB
```

Or call it from your terminal if you plan on adding it later on. As we'll see in no time, extended Globbing is there to give a special meaning to characters like #, which if you recall, is typically used for comments. Now let's get our hands dirty.

# Special patterns

Zsh's vast repertoire also includes a series of shortcuts or special patterns that aim to make mundane tasks a bit more tolerable. We will get familiarized with them in this section.

## Recursive searching

Arguably, the most popular pattern out there is recursive searching. Accessible through the **/ combination, this pattern tells zsh to perform a recursive search, starting from the current directory and working its way inwards along the directory tree.

For example, here's how we look for all the markdown files (files which typically have the .md extension) on the current working directory:

```
% echo **/*.md
README.md brew/README.md git/README.md scripts/README.md zsh/README.md
```

Then there's also the ***/ flavor, which tells the shell to follow symbolic links. Be careful though, as it can lead to errors such as "file name too long", which is the operating system's way of telling you that either the rabbit hole is too deep, or you have a circular reference somewhere.

> Keep in mind that specialized tools like find or The Silver Searcher (https://github.com/ggreer/the_silver_searcher) will run circles around the shell's directory recursion mechanism. Thus, you should avoid relying on it for "serious" operations.

As for the caveats of using the recursive pattern expression, you might eventually be greeted with an "argument list too long" warning from the system. This usually means the shell is taking up too much memory space when expanding the **/ pattern into the directory structure, which in turn could happen if you have a really complex tree to work on. A workaround, if you insist on using the recursive expansion, is to pass each argument with the help of xargs as follows:

```
% find **/*.md | xargs echo
```

I know, this example is a bit dumb as the same could be accomplished just with a simple find **/*.md for a multiple-row result. The idea here is that you get to know how to pipe the results of the find into echo by splitting them with xargs, so bear with me.

Lastly, there's somewhat of a hack you can use in case you want to exclude the current directory from the pattern:

```
% echo */**/*.md
```

That way, only filenames that include base_dir/any_dir will match the pattern.

## Alternate patterns

Having to choose between two options and then being given a third one clearly inferior, can make a person rethink his decision... or so the story goes. Luckily, the shell is not a complex creature like us, and we can provide it with a choice of patterns to select should one fail. We do that by using the parentheses with a pipe construct, like the following example:

```
% echo [[:upper:]]*.(md|txt)
README.md README.txt
```

We continue on our search for the README files, using a named range to specify the filename we want with an uppercase letter before defining either an md or a txt extension. Simple, right? Well, not quite. Just be careful so as not to start the command line with parentheses, as this might make them run in a subshell instead. Zsh is smart enough to discriminate between intended usages, so you'll probably be safe most of the time. Try not to push your luck though.

Before we move on, it bears mentioning you can't use a pattern that contains a / character within the group alternatives we just learned. You have been warned!

## Numeric ranges

You can make the shell match any series of digits it encounters with the < - > special pattern. What makes this construct great though, is that it can match any series of digits without a length restriction (this is because the shell processes each digit independently and not as a whole integer).

Take, for example, the following directory:

```
% ls
log.txt        log_002.txt  log_010.txt  log_031.txt
log_001.txt  log_009.txt  log_030.txt
```

We want to work with those files that match the log_xxx.txt pattern, where xxx is a digit. Let's put what we just learned to good use:

```
% echo log_<->.txt
log_001.txt log_002.txt log_009.txt log_010.txt log_030.txt log_031.txt
```

What if we want those logfiles from 10 upwards? Zsh has you covered:

```
% echo log_<10->.txt
log_010.txt log_030.txt log_031.txt
```

As you can see, the < - > pattern can define a range with lower and upper bounds. Let's try again, this time for files between 10 and 20:

```
% echo log_<10-20>.txt
log_010.txt
```

Another cool feat of this expression is that it doesn't take into account leading zeroes, allowing you to sort things such as `00010` and `00013`. Speaking of which, there's the `NUMERIC_GLOB_SORT` option, which you can also set in order to output a sorted numeric match of any pattern matches (and that's *any* as in, not just the numeric range pattern).

```
% setopt numericglobsort
% echo log_*
log_001.txt log_002.txt log_009.txt log_010.txt log_030.txt log_031.txt
```

# Revisiting the caret operator

As we saw earlier, we use the caret (^) operator to negate patterns (remember: "anything but what matches this"). Here's another way to use the caret:

```
% ls
README.md  README.txt  bindings.c  bindings.h  bindings.o  main.c  main.o


% echo b^*.o
bindings.c bindings.h
```

So basically, we're telling the shell to expand that pattern so as to match the filenames that start with `b` but do not have an `.o` extension.

We can then safely say that the `pattern^other_pattern` expressions work by matching the first pattern and avoiding matches on the `other_pattern` side of the expression. A word of caution now that we are using special characters with different meanings though is, remember to wrap names or expressions that you want taken literally with single quotes, like in the following example:

```
% echo '^c'
```

Otherwise, you might be asking for trouble.

# The tilde operator

Similar to the caret operator's second usage, the tilde (~) operator can be used to define a pattern that consists of a part that should match and a second part that shouldn't:

```
% ls
README.md  README.txt  bindings.c  bindings.h  bindings.o  main.c  main.o

% echo b*~*.o
bindings.c bindings.h
```

Basically, this is just a combination of two patterns: b* and *.o, linked with the "do not match what follows" operator: ~. Again, we can read that as "match everything that starts with a lowercase b and does not match anything that ends with .o".

If you recall, we used b^*.o with the caret, so the tilde version seems a bit more straightforward if I might say so. But don't take my word for it. Let's use the tilde to exclude, for example, any files within a temporary directory:

```
% ls tmp
delete_me.sh   out.txt

% echo **/*.sh~tmp/*
src/script.sh
```

What happens is that the shell runs the first pattern (**/*.sh) and recursively checks for all files with the sh extension. The preliminary result is a list of possible filenames that is then matched against the second pattern (tmp/*). The filenames that match the latter are removed from the list, and we are left with the filenames we were searching for.

Just for academic purposes, it might be a good time to mention that **/ is equivalent to the (*/)# pattern. As it stands, the special operator # will match a single repeating character (in parentheses), or a recurrent expression (in brackets).

# Glob qualifiers

Besides operators, zsh boasts qualifiers, which are essentially a sort of filters you apply to your pattern in order to restrict things like matching only files or folders, type of permissions for those filenames, or even the owner of such entries.

So in the following example, we'll list all the *directories* that match the *tmp pattern. Notice the (/) construct, that's what intuitively sets files and folders apart:

```
% echo *tmp(/)
tmp
```

What about matching only vanilla files then? Fair enough, (.) is your designed qualifier for files-only restrictions.

```
% ls -F
README.txt   script.zsh   zsh/   src/
```

Suddenly, a wild filename appears:

```
% echo *zsh(.)
script.zsh
```

We have a `zsh` directory and a script file with a `.zsh` extension. Typically, we would roll with an `echo *zsh` construct to list both of them, or a more restrictive `echo *.zsh` construct if we were just looking for files with an extension; however, the `(.)` qualifier is arguably better suited for complex tree searches or when dealing with lots of similar filenames and directories.

What follows is a "cheatsheet" for the most common qualifiers:

- `(N)`: Remove argument if no matches are found, silently ignore errors. Acts as a per-command `NO_GLOB` option.
- `(@)`: Symlink qualifier. Used for only selecting symbolic links.
- `(-@)`: A special variation of the previous one. Use this to find any *broken* symlinks.
- `(/)`: Directories only.
- `(.)`: Files only. Whatever is not either a link, directory, or any of the previous will be selected by this.
- `(*)`: Executable files. Directories need not apply. Think of this as `(.)` for those files with +x permissions.
- `(r)`: File is readable by the current shell user.
- `(w)`: File is writable by the current shell user.
- `(x)`: File is executable by the current shell user.
- `(U)`: File is owned by the current shell user.
- `(R)`: File is readable by anyone.
- `(W)`: File is writable by anyone.
- `(X)`: File is executable by anyone.
- `(u:root:)`: File is owned by the user `root`. You can replace the `:` character with any another pair of symbols such as curly braces: `(u{root})`. Just refrain from using pipes (`|`).
- `(on)`: Sort filenames by name. The `echo *(on)` construct will be analogous to `ls`.
- `(On)`: Reverse-sort filenames by name.
- `(oL)`: Sort filenames by file size.
- `(OL)`: Reverse-sort filenames by file size.
- `(om)`: Sort filenames by modification date.
- `(Om)`: Reverse-sort filenames by modification date.

As always, feel free to mix and match to spice up things. Like poking with (*r^w) for regular files that are readable but not writable by your user, or (@,/) for either symlinks or directories.

> Eager to find out more about qualifiers and what have you? Fret not dear reader, and embrace the mystical powers of... never mind, we'll just resort to *context completion*.
>
> Type the following, and remember to press *Tab* right after the opening parentheses:
>
> `% echo *zsh<Tab>`
>
> This will yield context completion for the glob qualifiers listed here (and many more!).

What follows are the more complex batch of qualifiers, such as timestamps and file size, which require a bit more explaining before delving right into their usage.

# Timestamp qualifiers

Unix systems typically record three timestamps on their filesystems: modification, access, and change times. With that in mind, you can use the following construct for Globbing filenames:

```
% echo *(mh-1)
```

This will provide you with the files modified in the last hour. You can easily check this result via an `ls -l` qualifier. The m there is the modification time, which is the most common type of timestamp you'll be interested in. Nevertheless, you could also check for either access ((ah-1)) or creation ((ch-1)) qualifiers within the last hour.

Regarding that "last hour" bit, it's represented by the h-1 qualifier, where h stands for hour (yes, yes, I know) and could be replaced by either minutes (m), weeks (w), or Months (an uppercase "M"). Note that the default unit for this qualifier is days, so (m-1) will mean a day ago or, more precisely, up to 24 hours before the current system time.

Similarly, the plus operator can be translated as "more than", allowing you to describe such patterns as (mw+3), which is a concise way of saying "more than three weeks from today". Finally, you can also specify a range by combining the two operators:

```
% echo *(m-5mh+2)
```

This will provide the files modified between five and two hours.

## File size qualifiers

The last qualifier you'll get to know today is the file size. As you might have guessed already, we can query filenames on the basis of their size on the disk:

- (Lm+size): The file size is larger than size megabytes. For example: (Lm+5) — larger than five megabytes.
- (Lm-size): The file is smaller than size megabytes. For example: (Lm-2) — smaller than two megabytes.
- (Lk+size): The file size is larger than size kilobytes. For example: (Lk+5000) — larger than 5000 kilobytes.
- (Lk-size): The file is smaller than size kilobytes. For example: (Lm-2000) — smaller than 2000 kilobytes.

# The zmv function

In the previous chapter, we learned about zle; zsh's module in charge of the command line. It's time we take advantage of our newly learned Globbing skills and get acquainted with zmv, a function that was created to make copying, moving, and linking files a breeze.

So, you ask, what's the deal with zmv? What's special about this built-in function in comparison to, say vanilla cp, is that zmv works its magic based on patterns. Further, as we'll see in this section, zmv is designed to be safe by default, which means it will ask you for a confirmation before taking on any kind of risky operation such as overwriting files.

Before we get started though, you should add the following to your .zshrc file, remembering to source it or restarting your terminal emulator of choice:

```
autoload zmv
```

This will make zsh load the function on startup, making it available to your session. You can now just type zmv and you'll be greeted with a fairly straightforward set of instructions. Basically, the zmv syntax expects two patterns: one for matching filenames and a second one into which the results will be converted:

```
zmv [OPTIONS] old_pattern new_pattern
```

As you might have guessed, zmv goes along with a great deal of Globbing, which is why we are only getting acquainted with it now. Here's how we can use it to rename our .txt files into markdown (.md):

```
% zmv -Wv '*.txt' '*.rb'
mv -- README.txt README.md
```

We used the verbose -v option flag, so we can learn more from the output. The zmv function works by expanding both patterns and then delegating the actual functionality to a more capable command such as cp, ln, or in this particular case, mv.

You can use the -W option to allow automatic conversion of the wildcards. Combined with noglob, you can add a brand new functionality to the mv command, which resembles the special behavior of the Windows systems' cmd variant:

```
alias mmv='noglob zmv -W'
```

You can now move files and rename them on the same call:

```
% mmv *.c.orig orig/*.c
```

As for the rest of the option flags that apply to zmv, here's a handful of the most relevant:

- -f: Force overwriting of destination files
- -i: Interactive prompt for each operation
- -n: No execution, just print what happens
- -v: Verbose — print a line as it is executed
- -w: Implicitly add parenthesis to wildcards in the pattern
- -W: Like -w, but turn wildcards in replacement patterns into references

However, don't even think you'll need to remember these. As we'll see in the next chapter, you can always use *Tab* for context completion or, in zmv's particular case, you can get the full list by simply typing zmv and pressing *Return* on your terminal. Just know there are at least a couple of options available to you.

> You can do what's popularly known as a dry run by passing the -n flag. This will make zmv only print out what will be done without actually doing it. This is by far the best way of testing and debugging your scripts before… well, you know, panic ensues.
>
> ```
> % ls foo
> % zmv -n '(*)' '${(U)1}''mv -- foo FOO
> ```

Should you require more advanced usage, you could use several expressions such as the old_pattern parameter. Filenames that match these will in turn be grouped and accessible by the new_pattern expression following the $1, $2, … pattern. For example, we can use the following for recursively renaming pictures on a folder tree so that their extensions are all lowercase:

```
% zmv '(**/)(*).(#i)jpg' '$1$2.jpg'
```

Summing up, with a bit of Globbing and practice, you can get a lot of mileage out of your zmv usage. You just need an appropriate pattern to match and a string to actually use that pattern. `zmv` will actually ignore any file whose name is not changed during expansion and it doesn't even care if the target is supposed to be a directory or a simple file.

> You can access zmv's advanced documentation by typing `man zshcontrib`.

# Summary

This is the part of our journey that requires us to pack up our things and wrap up the chapter. On this occasion though, we went from using Globbing as something we thought was "quite like a regular expression" to understanding what is actually a whole different beast. Luckily for us, that beast was pretty easy to tame once we learned the behavior of the most popular operators and qualifiers. We then expanded on those constructs with more special patterns and got to know **zmv** in order to make most of our daily tasks a breeze. Summing up, we can say that we:

- Learned about quotes, escaping symbols, and double quotes together with shell expansion within them

- Got started with Globbing and parameter substitution within the command line

- Kicked it up a notch and dove headfirst into extended Globbing, learning about recursive searching, and operators for negating and excluding patterns

- We learned about glob qualifiers, how to use them to discriminate files by the system time and size

- And finally discovered zmv, which lets us put all of the preceding things together to make working with complex filenames something like a walk in the park

Seems like we have seen a whole lot so far, which will cater to most of our needs. Not a bad deal, if I might say so. Actually, I might, as that's one of the advantages of wearing the writer's hat.

The next chapter covers completion. And we have come together quite well so far, so I won't lie to you (again); completion is actually what makes most people never look back once they try zsh. You have tasted a sample of it so far, but there's plenty more waiting for you, right around this page.

Next up then is *Chapter 5, Completion*. Hurry up!

# 5
# Completion

This is what most users switch to zsh for: completion. In this chapter, we'll meet one of the best features of zsh: `compsys`. Known as "the new" completion mechanism, this chapter focuses on its various functions and configuration. We will learn to tweak the completion behavior so that it's no longer restricted to filenames and bump it up using styles and our own functions. When we're done, you should be able to read most zsh scripts as well as tweak many of the existing functions.

## Getting started with completion

Nobody really likes to type boring filenames, and that's what got completion started back in the day — type a few letters of a filename, press *Tab*, and the shell will do the rest for you. Zsh goes the extra mile though and actually allows you to complete almost anything. By default, the *Tab* key is bound to a completion command in zsh.

Like Bash, zsh defaults to filename completion. Unlike anything else, however, zsh can enable the completion for practically everything that dares to rear its head in the command line — paths, external and built-in commands, aliases, functions, and options; you name it. And even if you can't name it, you can program it, as we will learn shortly.

Originally, zsh used a built-in module with a special syntax in order to provide completion. Luckily for us, this was eventually replaced by an even simpler mechanism. We'll focus on the new completion system that is entirely based on shell functions.

Go ahead and pop open that `.zshrc` file of yours, and add the following in order to activate shell completion:

```
autoload -U compinit
compinit
```

This addition will make the shell load the completion system and start it automatically. The `-U` flag tells the shell to avoid expanding any aliases. This will make double tapping *Tab* trigger the completion mode.

> `compinit` is an essential part of the completion system. As such, you won't be able to test anything from here on until you have updated and sourced your `.zshrc` file or at least run `autoload -U compinit && compinit` in your terminal.

Remember to source your files, and then let's go ahead and try our newly enabled completion. Type `ec` and press *Tab*:

```
% ec <Tab>
% echo
```

The shell automatically completes the external command as `echo`. How nice of zsh, isn't it?

> As we have previously noted, zsh has two ways of performing completions in the command line. You can learn more about "the old way" of doing things by typing `man zshcompctl`, for academic purposes, of course.

Completion can also be applied to environment variables, for example:

```
% echo $HOM <Tab>
% echo $HOME
```

By default, zsh enables the `AUTO_LIST` option that handles the resolution of ambiguous matches, providing you with all the possible completions. To see this in action, let's go back to the previous example; only this time, we will make the completion less obvious by typing only `HO` as follows:

```
% echo $HO<Tab>
Completing parameter
HOME  HOST
```

The shell doesn't know for sure what we mean, so it presents us with a list of possible matches below the prompt instead. This list will be updated if the criteria changes, so we need to only worry about hitting the *Tab* key.

Now, let's try option completion with `ls`, as follows:

```
% ls -<Tab>
```

The following screenshot shows you how completion is triggered for the
`ls` command:

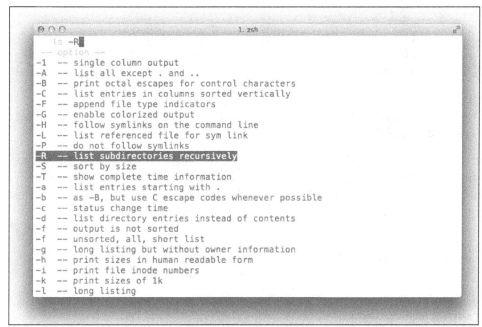

Menu selection in action

Seeing that there are actually a couple of viable options to pick from, zsh presents
you with a menu that you can cycle through by repeatedly hitting the *Tab* key or
using the arrow keys.

Finally, you can also use completion for expanding commands as follows:

```
% echo `which zsh`<Tab>
% echo /usr/local/bin/zsh
```

You can see where this is going—completion is awesome enough for us to want it to
be applied everywhere, and not just in the word that's being typed. Before we start
writing our own functions however, we will take a look at zsh styles, the options by
which we can configure the behavior of the `zstyle` built-in.

# Getting assertive with zstyle

Unlike the shell options that we have been setting—and unsetting—throughout this
book, zstyles demand a bit more complex syntax as a trade-off for enabling a context-
sensitive completion.

Zstyles are defined via the `zstyle` keyword, followed by a colon-delimited list of arguments:

```
:completion:function:completer:command:argument:tag
```

The first argument, `completion`, is used for defining a context, as any given style could behave differently in different contexts. Nothing to write home about though, as we'll get to see in no time.

The second argument is the name of the style by which it will be referenced by the built-in. The remainder of the arguments are what give the style their unique behavior for completion.

Patterns make a comeback here as well, so you can use them as tokens for each of the subsequent arguments when defining a style. As usual, order matters when you want to define your styles, so try to put the less-specific or general-purpose styles at the bottom of your definitions, otherwise you'll end up overriding your more-specific functions.

The most general type of style you can define is `:completion:*`, which will apply to almost anything, so be careful when ordering something that resembles it.

As you might have imagined, zsh has a few tricks up its sleeve, such as being capable of displaying some useful messages with the list of matches. For this to work though, we need to enable the following style:

```
zstyle ':completion:*' format %d
```

By adding this to your `.zshrc` file, you can now get a bit more information whenever zsh is performing a completion. For example:

```
% true<Tab>

no argument or option
```

The astute reader might have noticed the `%d` pattern lying within the style format. That's right, we can use the same escape sequences as that we used when defining our prompts.

> Tired of hearing beeps already? That's zsh's way of telling us that an ambiguous completion was attempted. You can put off this rather annoying attitude towards ambiguity by unsetting the `LIST_BEEP` option in your `.zshrc` file:
>
> ```
> unsetopt LIST_BEEP
> ```

As we mentioned earlier, you can also narrow down the behavior of your styles to a more specific context. For example, you could use any of the following:

```
zstyle ':completion:*:descriptions' format '%B%d%b'
zstyle ':completion:*:messages' format %d
zstyle ':completion:*:warnings' format 'No matches for: %d'
```

This is just to set a custom pattern for the messages belonging to warnings, messages, and descriptions groups. As you can see, warnings will now be reported as No matches for: <argument>, which is a bit less dronish.

You could also add a little more flair to your results with something along the following lines:

```
zstyle ':completion:*' group-name ''
```

This will display all the different types of matches separately. If no tag or group is defined for a particular match, it'll get displayed under the default group.

 Did the menu selection tickle your fancy? Here's how we make it available for all of your matches:

```
zstyle ':completion:*' menu select=1
```

Getting comfortable with the styles? Glad to hear. As you can see from the examples, there's no arcane magic involved here—just some documentation and creativity to fill the gap between you and your custom styles.

# Command correction

Completion can also correct any misspelled commands that you might have typed. We'll use the following format for our style:

```
zstyle ':completion:*' completer _expand _complete _correct
```

And we'll test the autocorrect functionality with the following:

```
% prnti<Tab>
corrections (2 errors)
print    printf
original
prnti
```

Zstyle noticed that we misspelled `print` and is being quite verbose regarding this. Remember you can use the *Tab* key to cycle through the list of available options.

Alternatively, you could use the `correct` option if you want a more "hold me by the hand" approach. Specifically, this option will make zsh ask you for confirmation every time it suggests a correction:

```
% setopt correct
% prnti<Tab>
zsh: correct 'prnti' to 'print' [nyae]?
```

This peculiar `nyae` acronym stands for *No, Yes, Abort,* and *Edit,* and works in the following way:

- n: This will force the shell to execute whatever you typed in the command line (prnti in this particular case).

- y: This will execute the correction (effectively, changing prnti to **print** in this example).

- a: This will abort and allow you to type a completely different command. Think of it as a panic button.

- e: This will allow you to edit the current text in the command line. Use this for a more fine-grained control in case suggestions made by the shell are completely off.

What about command options? You know, those flags we pass around all the time? Well, turns out there is a style for that too. The following will make the commands show the descriptions for their options:

```
zstyle ':completion:*' verbose yes
```

These can be easily accounted for; now, go ahead and type the following:

```
% print -<Tab>

-- option --
-C  -- print arguments in specified number of columns
-D  -- substitute any arguments which are named directories using ~
notation
-N  -- print arguments separated and terminated by nulls
-O  -- sort arguments in descending order
(list goes on...)
```

Not too shabby, right? Remember how I mentioned we wouldn't be in such a dire need for manpages after we learned some styles? No? Well, we won't be in such... never mind.

# Completers

The third entry on the zstyle is reserved for completers. These are the functions that handle the different types of completions available. By default, the list of completers consists of a single function, _complete, but each member of the completers family will add its own unique behavior to your styles.

```
zstyle ':completion:*' completer _expand _complete _correct
```

Used in your .zshrc file, this completer will use globbing for expanding the input and match it against the _complete and _correct completers. The _correct completer is used here for correcting any typos and spelling mistakes. We're leaving it at the end of the argument list so that _complete takes precedence.

> When used within a style, completer names omit the leading underscore:
>
> ```
> zstyle ':completion::complete:*' use-cache on
> ```
>
> This style configures the _complete completer by enabling a cache layer for any completions that require it, improving the overall responsiveness of such functions.

Similar to _correct, _approximate will carry out the same tasks with the added benefit of allowing a few extra characters to be misspelled at the cursor position. Notice that you will need to put _approximate before _correct, should you need to use both in your style.

As a function, zstyle also uses flags. Of particular interest to us is the -e option, which tells zstyle to evaluate the final string as an argument on each call. This allows us to use more dynamic styles such as the following:

```
# One error for every three characters
zstyle -e ':completion:*:approximate:*' max-errors 'reply=( $((
  ($#PREFIX+$#SUFFIX)/3 )) numeric )'
```

This configures the approximate completer to evaluate the argument for the max-errors parameter dynamically, each time it is invoked. The reply=( $(( ($#PREFIX+$#SUFFIX)/3 )) numeric ) string uses the reply hook for displaying the results within the line editor and sets its value as the expression, (PREFIX + SUFFIX)/3. This is our way of saying "one error for every three characters". Both PREFIX and SUFFIX are variables that contain the values before and after the cursor position, respectively.

# Ignoring matches

Sometimes, some matching suggestions jump out at you as being completely out of place. Luckily for us, the developers of zsh have included an _ignore completer.

Take the following directory tree as an example:

```
zsh
├── README.md
├── Completion/
├── Misc/
├── Scripts/
└── Util/
```

When working on any of the subdirectories mentioned previously—for example, the Completion folder—see what happens when we try to change directory, using cd, to another at the same level:

```
% cd ../ <Tab>
directory
Completion/
Misc/
Scripts/
Util/
```

Having the Completion mechanism display the folder we're currently located in is a bit awkward, and it makes the whole cd deal a bit pointless. In order to make the shell a bit more context-sensitive, we can alter the completion behavior for the cd command using the ignore-parents, parent, and pwd options:

```
zstyle ':completion:*:cd:*' ignore-parents parent pwd
```

The following will remove the respective matches from the completion results. Notice how Completion is now missing from the results:

```
% cd ../ <Tab>
directory
Misc/
Scripts/
Util/
```

While we're at it, you can use the following style to remove the trailing slash when using a directory as an argument:

```
zstyle ':completion:*' squeeze-slashes true
```

# Function definitions

Finally, we will turn our attention to compsys, zsh's completion system. This is one of the most complex parts of the shell for users and developers alike. Before we dive into compsys, however, we need to make a quick stop and meet an actual function in the wild.

 As usual, you can learn more about compsys via the manpages. Of particular interest are man zshcompsys and man zshcompwid.

Here's what one of these looks like:

```
hi() {
print 'Hello, world'
}
```

Here, we have defined the hi function, which is how we'll call it again later when we need it. This will, in turn, print Hello, world every time we use it. So let's get to it, shall we?

Open your terminal emulator of choice, and type the following (one line at a time):

```
% hi() {
function> print 'Hello, World!'
function> }
```

Notice how zsh realized this was indeed a function we were trying to define and immediately used the continuation prompt (function>), allowing you to continue working on it? How nice of zsh to wait for us until we properly close our curly braces.

Now, go ahead and test your first function:

```
% hi
Hello, World!
```

They grow so fast!

And, now for the sad part—this was defined for your current session only, just like when we defined aliases back in *Chapter 2, Alias and History*, at the beginning of our zsh adventure. If you want hi(), or any other function to tag along in each interactive session of yours, you'll need to add it to your startup files.

A word of advice though: once you start with the completion and functions, these startup files will get pretty crowded. So, it's probably best that you start relocating your functions into a more comfy space like their own .zsh_functions file. Fret not, as the process is easy.

First, we create a hidden file; you can name it whatever you fancy, but we'll go with .zsh_functions (see the leading dot, so we can tell the system that it can hide it).

```
% touch ~/.zsh_functions
```

Once you have created the file in your $HOME directory, it's simply a matter of adding your functions in here. You can use your favorite editor; we'll just roll with cat here for convenience:

```
% cat >> ~/.zsh_functions
greet() {
  print 'Hello, World!'
}
```

Press *Ctrl + D* to close the file.

Now, as we learned previously, this wouldn't do anything by itself unless we source the file. And since sourcing the file manually in each session would be a pain in the neck, we just need to go a step further and add the .zsh_functions sourcing to our startup files. So, go ahead and open your .zshrc file, and add the following:

```
[[ -f ~/.zsh_functions ]] && source ~/.zsh_functions
```

This is a conditional statement. The double square braces ([[) shown here are known as the test command (or *new test* if you have been around the command line for a while), and they help you compare strings and test for file attributes. The -f switch is for regular files and succeeds only if the file exists. So we're literally trying to say "test whether the ~/.zsh_functions file exists". If the test passes, the following part of the command will get chained and we'll finally source our functions file.

As a side note, this expression supports filename globbing, so all the tricks we learned in *Chapter 4, Globbing*, still apply here.

You can source as many files as you like with this same mechanism; just remember to add the line into your .zshrc file, and don't forget about the test fail-switch, which will avoid sourcing files that do not exist in the system (and of course, errors).

As always, you can scuba dive into the test command simply by typing man [ in your terminal. For more details regarding the [[ compound command, check the *CONDITIONAL EXPRESSIONS* section under the zshmisc(1) manual entry.

Okay, I hear you. So what do functions have to do with completion? Well, everything! See, compsys is entirely made out of functions: functions that will be called automatically whenever you hit the *Tab* key. The difference lies in how these set of functions use some other special commands to interact with our old pal, ZLE, in order to show the available completions. Don't worry though; contrary to popular belief, there's no arcane magic in here.

# The path of the function

So, functions. A truckload of them to be more precise (well, you be the judge of this). How does zsh know where to look? It is easier than it sounds; the shell will load anything that belongs to its function path or $fpath, a series of directories that contain the files with the functions required for completion. Go ahead and have a look at it:

```
% print -l $fpath
```

All the directories that show up in your function path list will be scanned and loaded by the shell during startup, provided you call compinit first. So remember to call autoload -U compinit in your .zshrc file. Note, however, that call will load anything that resides in your $fpath. If you happen to have a special requirement for a single function, you could call it explicitly via autoload. If you save the previous function as a file named _greet and put it into one of the directories within your $fpath, you could then use the following inside your startup files for loading the function into the shell automatically:

```
% cat >> _greet
echo 'Hello world!'


autoload -Uz _greet
```

See that -Uz flag? The -U flag works by telling the shell to use the name _greet to refer to the function we just created, whereas the -z flag tells zsh to load the function in the native mode. Both -U and -z flags are always added implicitly whenever you call autoload, but I'm leaving it there for you to be aware of them.

Okay, so it's all fun and single-line functions until someone needs something a bit more complex. Single functions within a file will be loaded without any problem whatsoever. So, how do we use helper functions (auxiliary methods for our main functionality) in our files? The zsh way states that we should define a function and name it just like the file and call it in the last line of the file:

```
_greet() {
    echo "Hello, World!"
}

_meet() {
    _greet
    echo "Ohai there $@"
}


_meet "$@"
```

That last line in the file takes care of calling the function named `_foo` inside the file, and passing it the same arguments used. So if you called it `meet John`, the arguments will be passed to the `meet` function.

Save the file as `meet` (no extension) inside any of your `$fpath` folders; restart your shell and call the following:

```
% meet John
Hello, World!
Ohai there john
```

**Extending your fpath**

If you don't want to be messing around with copies or links to your functions, you can easily extend `fpath` with more folders by setting the variable as follows:

```
fpath=(~/my_folder $fpath)
```

This will prepend the folder, `my_folder`, to the shell's `fpath`, effectively extending it with whatever lies inside your folders. This is particularly useful for those times when you lack the appropriate permissions on a given system. Note that we are using the absolute path to the folder.

So let's take a look at a formal completion function. Don't worry, we'll start with an easy one, such as _md5sum, which is typically located under your $ZSH_INSTALL_DIR/functions/ folder. Here it lies in all its glory:

```
#compdef md5sum

_arguments -S \
    '(-b --binary)'{-b,--binary}'[read in binary mode]' \
    '(-c --check)'{-c,--check}'[read MD5 sums from the FILEs and check
them]' \
    '(-t --text)'{-t,--text}'[read in text mode]' \
    '--status[no output, status code shows success]' \
    '(-w --warn)'{-w,--warn}'[warn about improperly formatted checksum
lines]' \
    '--help[display help and exit]' \
    '--version[output version information and exit]' \
    '*:files:_files'
```

Go ahead and test this by typing md5sum - followed by pressing the *Tab* key, and you'll be prompted with the options from arguments.

Your very first line of code in any completion function must be the #compdef clause, followed by the name of the program to be completed by the function (md5sum, in this particular case).

Next up is a call to the internal _arguments function, which does the actual handling of the options to be formatted and displayed on screen. This function is typically used when specifying the completion of commands whose arguments follow standard Unix conventions in their options and arguments' lists. Using the -S option, we declare that no option will be completed after -- shows up on the line. This is the delimiter used to end the parsing of the option, so this argument would be typically ignored unless we explicitly say otherwise.

If you look closely though, you'll notice that each of the argument entries (split into continuation lines via \) follows the same pattern:

```
'(optional exclusion list)'{options}'[help text in brackets]'
```

Note that the curly braces around the option and its verbose variant are there to group them together, otherwise they are optional.

The exclusion list works by explicitly telling zsh what should not be included in the results. In other words, whenever the option parameter is typed, hide all the other options from (exclusions). Take for example the following line:

```
'(-t --text)'{-t,--text}'[read in text mode]'
```

If `-t` or `--text` appears in the command line, do not show the `-t` or `--text` options as completions.

This makes even more sense for commands such as `ln`, where you want to avoid offering some potentially misguiding options:

```
'(-L -P)-H[with -R, follow symlinks on the command line]'
```

Hide the options `-L` and `-P` if `-H` is being used; this is because both the options are used for "always follow symbolic links" and "never follow symbolic links", respectively.

Finally, there's the last line of the `_md5sum` function:

```
'*:files:_files'
```

This uses the `_files` helper function that is somewhat the standard tool for completing filenames. With this line, we make sure that filenames are completed even if no other options' flags are suggested.

Moreover, `_files` uses an additional function, `_path_files`, and passes its arguments to the latter. On its own, `_path_files` is the de facto function for completing filenames within the completion system. As if it wasn't enough, `_path_files` has some really handy tricks up its sleeve such as completion of partial paths, which enables things such as `/u/bi/zs` to be completed to `/usr/bin/zsh`.

Then, there are also helper functions such as `_call_program`, which are used to execute any kind of commands available to the system. A common practice when using `_call_program` is to redirect the standard error to `/dev/null` (this is a nice way of saying it's silencing any error-induced screams) and allows us to save the output of the command into a variable.

And that's all there's to it. Well, at least for getting started with the completion mechanism and custom-made functions. Although, on some occasions, getting your hands dirty and extending the completion system with your own functions will only get you so far, this quick fly-by should be enough to get you excited about the possibilities lying there. Again, it's advisable that you try not to reinvent the wheel — as we'll see in the next chapter, there are many other projects out there that can give you a nice boost in the completion department.

You can now go ahead and take a deep dive into the `functions` folder of your zsh installation to start getting familiarized with the thousands of lines of code there. Who knows? Perhaps the starting template for the next completion function is just waiting there for you.

# Summary

We are almost done with this adventure, and it seems you are now more ready than ever to start tackling major annoyances like your favorite program not having a set of completion definitions. Even better, you can tweak and improve the existing functionality, which otherwise would make your work really frustrating.

Besides writing your own functions, we also learned how to tweak the shell behavior and go a step above filename completion. With a bit of practice and further tweaking, you can now become a real speed demon of the command line. Best of all, it only takes a couple of *Tab* presses to get there.

Summing it up, here's what's covered in this chapter:

- The types of completion available to zsh — zstyles and functions, which allow you to customize the behavior of the completion mechanism and extend its functionality
- The different types of completers (particularly `correct`, `approximate` & `ignore`) and their role when defining zstyles
- A few tips for creating and extending your our own completion functions

Okay then, before I get sentimental, we should hurry to the next chapter that has a few suggestions before we're done with this journey of ours.

# 6
# Tips and Tricks

So, this is where we part ways. We have come a long way since defining our first alias, so there's really not much left for us to discover, at least not with the number of pages left for us. Like a nosy neighbor though, I can't help but give you a few more tips before our journey ends.

## Main resources

Hold your horses there buddy. Before you start typing down tips and tweaking your configuration, it's important that I point you towards zsh's official site once again. Zsh's page is located at `http://www.zsh.org`, and you can take your browser there to take a look at the *Frequently Asked Questions* section as well as other interesting entries such as **Scripts & contributions**. Turns out this is our main source of information for our new favorite shell, so I recommend you refer it to keep up with changes between releases and the awesome user guides and manuals located there.

Perhaps the most feature-packed item on the list of recommendations is the zsh wiki (`http://zshwiki.org`). There you will find a lot of useful information about zsh together with tips and user-suggested configurations. Overall an excellent starting point for stuffing your startup files to the gills. It's worth noting that this is a user-maintained site, which means you can contribute to it by submitting your own configurations and scripts as well as editing existing content.

No project with the magnitude of zsh is without its mailing list. You can find zsh's located at `http://www.zsh.org/mla` and have a look at the thousands of interesting discussions going on for more tips, tricks, and announcements that happen around the project. Remember, you can also use this for any impending questions you have regarding the shell and the project in general. Also an excellent starting point if you are looking forward to contributing to the project.

Finally, for those inclined to "group chat", there's an IRC channel hosted on **freenode** (`http://freenode.net`) as `#zsh`. This is your go-to source to get help and discuss zsh with lots of other users.

# Helping tips

What follows is a list of "nice things to have" on your configuration files, aliases, and functions. Think of these as a helping hand with some of the more boring tasks that involve the command line.

# Directory substitution

This is one of the cooler tricks you can pull with zsh, albeit a bit hidden from plain sight. Did you know you can use `cd` for switching between parallel directories without even typing the whole path? Let's work with an example.

Say you were located in the directory `/zsh/completion/unix/`; now, see the following command:

```
% cd completion doc
```

This command would effectively move your current working directory to `/zsh/doc/unix/`, provided both the directories have the same tree structure and are located on the same branch level. I know, I too can't imagine myself living without it.

Remember, you can set the `AUTOCD` option to enable `cd` just by typing the name of a directory, provided that the directory exists and is not an ambiguous match, of course.

# Magic space

It's safe to assume that you have been using the *Tab* key for completion so far, but the shell also provides a `magic-space` functionality that is really worth being bound to your space bar. Simply add the following code to your `.zshrc` file:

```
bindkey ' ' magic-space
```

And try typing something followed immediately by the space bar as follows:

```
% echo !!<Space>
```

You'll notice what that "magic" means right away, as pressing the space bar now triggers history expansion on the current line.

# Random numbers

I've lost track of how many times I needed an actual random number in order to fill in a form or make a completely arbitrary decision, just like those times you can't decide between cappuccino or latte.

Let's borrow a helping hand from our friend $RANDOM and sprinkle some arithmetic expansion on top. Putting everything together, we end up with the following alias:

```
alias rand='echo $(( ( RANDOM % 10 ) + 1 ))'
```

What this does is uses the $RANDOM internal function to get a *pseudorandom* number for us. We then use the *modulo* operator (%) to get the remainder of the division by 10; this way, we can get only numbers between 1 and 10. The 1 being added that you see is there because the 1 to 10 range is actually interpreted by your computer as "0-9", which includes the first 10 digits, but is a bit less human friendly.

The whole expression is wrapped with the arithmetic expansion construction $(()) that we learned about in *Chapter 2, Alias and History*, and allows us to operate with numbers such as $RANDOM.

You can now go ahead and type rand every time you need an actual random number output on your terminal window.

As a side note, keep in mind that, as with all things computer-generated, there's no such thing as a purely "random" event—unless you are talking to my boss about one of my bugs. Those are completely random phenomena—so don't rely on this for security or sensitive operations.

# zcalc

Most times, math just catches us with an unfairly low caffeine level. Attempting algebra at those times usually calls for a quick calculator. Turns out zsh comes packed with just one of those.

The way it works is similar to the tetris and zle modules; just add autoload -Uz zcalc to your .zshrc and type zcalc on your terminal emulator whenever the need arises. To exit zcalc just press *Ctrl + D*.

# Change and list directory contents

Like many, many other users of shells out there, most of of the time with shell you will be switching between directories and listing their contents. It's reasonable to assume that during your normal workflow, you'll be calling cd and ls quite a lot.

Look at the following example:

```
% cd some_dir
> ~/gfestari/somedir/
% ls
> file1.txt  file2.txt
```

Fret not, dear reader, you are not alone. Most fellow shell users feel your pain. Luckily, there's something we can do about it, which involves a simple function to change our current working directory with cd and then calling ls to list the contents of the new directory as shown in the following code snippet:

```
# calls cd, and immediately list its contents
function cs {
    cd "$@" && ls -A
}
```

Our new cs function will perform just like cd, but will list the contents of any directory we move to. The $@ string you see there is the current command arguments we use when calling cs. These get passed in its entirety to cd, so we don't need to worry about handling them with the same finesse as the actual program. We then use the double ampersand logic operator && (read that as "and") to chain the ls command with the -A option. This works as "execute cd and if it succeeds, call ls -A".

Put this on your startup files, and start changing directories by typing cs.

# Finding your path through commands

We have used which many times already throughout this book, but it's time for you to learn about yet another cool zsh feature, courtesy of the command substitution mechanism: the =command shortcut.

Try the following command line, which should point you towards zsh's binary location:

```
% echo $(which zsh)
> /usr/local/bin/zsh
```

And now, let's try using the equivalent shortcut:

```
% echo =zsh
> /usr/local/bin/zsh
```

This will work the same as which with a lot less typing as long as you remember to follow that equals sign immediately with the name of any program on your system.

# Other projects

This section aims to point you towards some of the most interesting projects and resources out there. The whole point of these is to have something of an "extra spice" to add your zsh.

## zsh-lovers

The `zsh-lovers` project (`http://grml.org/zsh/zsh-lovers.html`) is a collection of useful tips, tricks, and examples that can be installed as a manual page and accessed from the terminal. One of the more interesting features of the project is the collection of examples for many of the "hidden"—or not so evident—features of zsh. Worth every byte, if only for the hundreds of hours of online searching it'll save you.

## zsh-users

The zsh users' repository on GitHub (`https://github.com/zsh-users`) packs a lot of incredibly useful code. Of particular interest to any zsh user are the projects `zsh-syntax-highlighting` (`https://github.com/zsh-users/zsh-syntax-highlighting`) and `zsh-history-substring-search` (`https://github.com/zsh-users/zsh-history-substring-search`).

As the name implies, `zsh-syntax-highlighting` offers syntax highlighting similar to that available in the fish shell, whereas `zsh-history-substring-search` again borrows a page from the fish's functionality and does a history search by allowing you to type any part of a history entry and press the up or down arrow keys to cycle through the matching commands.

Also available on the zsh users' repository is the `zsh-completions` project (`https://github.com/zsh-users/zsh-completions`), a collection of community-submitted completion functions for a lot of popular programs and tools such as Node.js, Redis, and Vagrant.

## oh-my-zsh

Unless you have been offline for the past couple of years, chances are you have already heard about oh-my-zsh (`https://github.com/robbyrussell/oh-my-zsh`). The community-driven project has helped zsh become incredibly popular by simplifying the initial configuration and learning curve for zsh. The framework packs more than a hundred plugins for tools like Ruby on Rails, Git, and Ant, and another chock-full of prompt themes; so the command line never gets boring.

# Prezto

Prezto (`https://github.com/sorin-ionescu/prezto`) is another popular project with some great configuration options. Like oh-my-zsh, Prezto packs what it calls "sane defaults", a handful of interesting aliases and functions together with autocompletion and—you guessed it—prompt themes.

Okay, I heard that. Does my shell *really need a framework?* Truth is you probably don't need *the whole package* but just a particular functionality, be it a completion function or prompt style. So why reinvent the wheel when someone has already thought about the problem and come up with a—hopefully elegant—solution? What I'm trying to say here is: look at the source code, see what you can bring into your configuration, and if you feel like it, give it back to the community. The next guy will surely appreciate it a lot.

# Explain Shell

Although not purely zsh-related, the Explain Shell project (`http://explainshell.com`) aims to lend a helping hand on those incredibly awkward commands by providing a really neat interface in which to parse and explain them term-by-term. This can prove really useful when experimenting with unfamiliar commands or things found in the strangest depths of the web.

# Your dotfiles

Noticed how your program's configuration files all are hidden by default? Even your startup files and zsh-related configuration lay on your home directory tucked away from plain sight by a leading dot on their filename. Commonly referred to as *dotfiles*, there are a lot of really cool settings and configurations out there that started as someone's clever attempt at fixing an annoyance. So go ahead and publish your dotfiles for the world to see. Turns out sharing your configuration is a really nice way of helping other users on their zsh adventures and getting feedback on what you have been so passionately working on. Just be careful not to share any passwords or credentials while you're at it!

If there's a book that should be on your radar after reading this, that should be *From Bash to Z Shell Conquering the Command Line* by *Oliver Kiddle, Peter Stephenson*, and *Jerry Peek*. An almost-instant classic for both beginners and power-users that will definitely help you expand your knowledge of the command line.

# Summary

And that brings us to the end of this book. Notice how I wrote "book" and not journey, as hopefully this first dip into zsh has gotten you excited enough about the possibilities of the shell and how versatile a tool it really is.

What now, then? Well, fortunately, that's up to you, dear reader. There's plenty more left on zsh for you to unravel and many more of those annoying and boring tasks that are required of your scripts, so you can go back to those other, important things on the backlog.

With a bit of spit and polish, particularly on the configuration side of things, zsh can really shine and make your life easier—and why not, fun—on the command line. So go ahead and get back to it. You'll be glad you did.

# Index

# Z

## Thank you for buying
# Learning Shell Scripting with Zsh

## About Packt Publishing

Packt, pronounced 'packed', published its first book "*Mastering phpMyAdmin for Effective MySQL Management*" in April 2004 and subsequently continued to specialize in publishing highly focused books on specific technologies and solutions.

Our books and publications share the experiences of your fellow IT professionals in adapting and customizing today's systems, applications, and frameworks. Our solution based books give you the knowledge and power to customize the software and technologies you're using to get the job done. Packt books are more specific and less general than the IT books you have seen in the past. Our unique business model allows us to bring you more focused information, giving you more of what you need to know, and less of what you don't.

Packt is a modern, yet unique publishing company, which focuses on producing quality, cutting-edge books for communities of developers, administrators, and newbies alike. For more information, please visit our website: www.packtpub.com.

## About Packt Open Source

In 2010, Packt launched two new brands, Packt Open Source and Packt Enterprise, in order to continue its focus on specialization. This book is part of the Packt Open Source brand, home to books published on software built around Open Source licences, and offering information to anybody from advanced developers to budding web designers. The Open Source brand also runs Packt's Open Source Royalty Scheme, by which Packt gives a royalty to each Open Source project about whose software a book is sold.

## Writing for Packt

We welcome all inquiries from people who are interested in authoring. Book proposals should be sent to author@packtpub.com. If your book idea is still at an early stage and you would like to discuss it first before writing a formal book proposal, contact us; one of our commissioning editors will get in touch with you.

We're not just looking for published authors; if you have strong technical skills but no writing experience, our experienced editors can help you develop a writing career, or simply get some additional reward for your expertise.

## Mastering HTML5 Forms

ISBN: 978-1-78216-466-1    Paperback: 148 pages

Create dynamic and responsive web forms with this in-depth, hands-on guide

1. Enhance the look and feel of your form

2. Optimize your user experience for any device

3. Utilize HTML5's brand new form elements

## Learning Bing Maps API

ISBN: 978-1-78355-037-1    Paperback: 116 pages

Obtain geographical data from Bing Maps and display them on the map

1. Display address information for any point on the map through the location-based REST services API

2. Embed a map on a web page with a custom theme

4. Geocode with Spatial Data APIs and display the information on the map

Please check **www.PacktPub.com** for information on our titles